Focusing and Calming Games for Children

by the same author

Anger Management Games for Children
Deborah M. Plummer
Illustrated by Jane Serrurier
ISBN 978 1 84310 628 9
eISBN 978 1 84642 775 6

Social Skills Games for Children
Deborah M. Plummer
Foreword by Professor Jannet Wright
Illustrated by Jane Serrurier
ISBN 978 1 84310 617 3
eISBN 978 1 84642 836 4

Self-Esteem Games for Children
Deborah M. Plummer
Illustrated by Jane Serrurier
ISBN 978 1 84310 424 7
eISBN 978 1 84642 574 5

Helping Children to Cope with Change, Stress and Anxiety
A Photocopiable Activities Book
Deborah M. Plummer
Illustrated by Alice Harper
ISBN 978 1 84310 960 0
eISBN 978 0 85700 366 9

Helping Children to Improve their Communication Skills
Therapeutic Activities for Teachers, Parents and Therapists
Deborah M. Plummer
Illustrated by Alice Harper
ISBN 978 1 84310 959 4
eISBN 978 0 85700 502 1

Helping Children to Build Self-Esteem
A Photocopiable Activities Book
2nd edition
Deborah M. Plummer
Illustrated by Alice Harper
ISBN 978 1 84310 488 9
eISBN 978 1 84642 609 4

Helping Adolescents and Adults to Build Self-Esteem
A Photocopiable Resource Book
Deborah M. Plummer
ISBN 978 1 84310 185 7
eISBN 978 1 84642 051 1

The Adventures of the Little Tin Tortoise
A Self-Esteem Story with Activities for Teachers, Parents and Carers
Deborah M. Plummer
Illustrated by Jane Serrurier
ISBN 978 1 84310 406 3
eISBN 978 1 84642 465 6

Focusing and Calming Games for Children

Mindfulness Strategies and Activities to Help Children Relax, Concentrate and Take Control

Deborah M. Plummer

Illustrated by Jane Serrurier

Jessica Kingsley *Publishers*
London and Philadelphia

First published in 2012
by Jessica Kingsley Publishers
116 Pentonville Road
London N1 9JB, UK
and
400 Market Street, Suite 400
Philadelphia, PA 19106, USA

www.jkp.com

Library of Congress Cataloging in Publication Data
Plummer, Deborah.
Focusing and calming games for children : mindfulness strategies and activities to help children to relax, concentrate and take control / Deborah M. Plummer ; illustrated by Jane Serrurier.
p. cm.
Includes bibliographical references.
ISBN 978-1-84905-143-9 (alk. paper)
1. Meditation for children. 2. Stress management for children. 3. Attention in children. I. Title.
BF723.M37P58 2012
155.4'189042--dc23
2012020911

British Library Cataloguing in Publication Data
A CIP catalogue record for this book is available from the British Library

ISBN 978 1 84905 143 9
eISBN 978 0 85700 344 7

Printed and bound in Great Britain

Contents

List of games

Acknowledgements

This book is one of a series based on the use of games to enhance social and emotional well-being (see *Self-Esteem Games for Children*, *Anger Management Games for Children*, *Helping Children to Cope with Change, Stress and Anxiety* and *Social Skills Games for Children*, all published by Jessica Kingsley Publishers). As with previous books, the games and activities in Part Two have been selected from several sources. Most have been collected or devised during 20 years or more of working as a therapist with children with speech, language and communication needs; some are adaptations of games contributed by children themselves during participation in therapy groups. There are also versions of activities that I have learnt on various training courses. My thanks therefore go to all the facilitators, teachers, therapists and children who have shared their ideas with me.

In researching appropriate games for this series, I have also found books by Penny Warner (*Kids' Party Games and Activities*), Mildred Masheder (*Let's Play Together*), Donna Brandes and Howard Phillips (*Gamesters' Handbook*), Arnold Arnold (*The World Book of Games*) and Marian Liebmann (*Art Therapy for Groups*) to be particularly useful, and for this book in particular I have used *Let's Play Asian Games* (Dunn 1978) as a source of ideas. This book, first published in 1978 by the Asian Cultural Centre for UNESCO, outlines several variations of different games and, in so doing, illustrates the universality of games of skill and imagination.

Thank you also to Doctor Roshan Rai, lecturer at De Montfort University, for his helpful comments on the section regarding developmental aspects of attention and concentration.

Note: The pronouns 'he' and 'she' have been used alternately throughout the book to refer to a child of either gender.

Part One

Theoretical and Practical Background

1

Introduction: Meeting Children with Mindfulness

Focusing and Calming Games for Children brings together a selection of games and ideas aimed at promoting a child's capacities to focus his attention, sustain concentration and calm himself both physically and mentally.

The book is based on the child-centred principles of the previous titles in this series (*Self-Esteem Games for Children, Anger Management Games for Children* and *Social Skills Games for Children*, all published by Jessica Kingsley Publishers). It draws together the principles of childhood well-being and mindful interactions outlined in these earlier books and crystallises them into a model of interaction that I have termed Mindfulness Play. This approach advocates mindfulness as a way of interaction in everyday life. It is an approach that involves heightening our own self-awareness and ability to be fully 'present' from moment to moment as well as nurturing this capacity in children.

Sogyal Rinpoche describes the practice of mindfulness as 'bringing the scattered mind home, and so of bringing the different aspects of our being into focus... In that settling we begin to understand ourselves more...' In mindfulness we view emotions and thoughts 'with an acceptance and generosity that are as open and spacious as possible' (Rinpoche 1995 p.61). In other words, mindfulness is about being open to whatever we encounter in this awakened relationship with ourselves and others.

Mindfulness Play has at its heart the idea that self-awareness and awareness of others does not need to be hard work, but that the attitude with which we engage in these games and activities and the context in which we undertake them are of paramount importance. A child's ability to attend to (be mindful of) his inner world of images and ideas is as important for his well-being as his ability to pay attention to the outer world. Similarly, we can be most effective in nurturing a child's well-being if we also have the ability to be attentive, patient and self-aware in our interactions. We may not always get it right, but the invaluable outcome of working in this way will be that children will learn to respect themselves, to trust their feelings and to believe in their abilities in ways that teaching specific skills and strategies alone will rarely achieve.

Games provide a fun way of learning serious ideas and important life skills. When they are facilitated by adults, they should always be played mindfully and with integrity. We need to be fully aware of why we are playing the games that we have chosen, fully conscious of the possible effects that playing such games might have and fully 'present' with the children in order to understand their ways of responding and interacting with each other and to appreciate their many, and often extraordinary, insights.

Being mindful in our interactions and developing our understanding of the child's perspective doesn't mean that we need to enter his world so fully that we lose sight of our role as mentor, facilitator or teacher, however. Neither should we remain attentive observers from a distance – a scientific stance that could all too easily lead us to judge a child's behaviour from our own viewpoint and perhaps urge us to teach him how he 'ought' to behave, think and feel in accordance with our adult understanding of life, or perhaps even in accordance with our knowledge of child development ('He *ought* to be able to do this/know this by now!').

There are, however, many opportunities open to us for joining with the children in our care in shared activities which bridge the diverse worlds of adults and children. It is often in those very special, almost magical moments of shared attention that insight and change take place (for children and adults alike), allowing children to become more autonomous and effective in their thinking and behaviour, and more in touch with life's joys and wonders.

The context of the games and activities described in this book is therefore the creation of this special meeting place, where the foundation elements for well-being and the skills involved in focusing and calming can develop and flourish in Mindfulness Play.

A meeting of such importance in shared territory can be fun but also a little daunting and potentially chaotic. Chapter 2 – 'Understanding Attention and Concentration' – therefore gives a brief theoretical perspective, outlining what we currently know about the developmental and neurocognitive aspects of attention control. Chapter 3 – 'Mindfulness Play' – sets the context for the games and activities, revisiting the importance of learning through play and of enhancing children's capacity to imagine. The suggestions in Chapter 4 – 'Structuring the Emotional Environment for Mindfulness Play' – highlight the need for careful consideration of how we interact with children during adult-directed play.

Having established the general layout of the territory, Chapter 5 – 'Mindfulness Play and Well-Being' – and Chapter 6 – 'Control, Adaptability and Effectiveness' – show how focusing, concentrating and self-calming are vital to well-being and how we can use specific strategies to enhance these components of our lives.

In Part Two (Chapters 7–12) the games and activities are divided into topic sections: choosing groups, pairs, leaders and order of play; warm-ups; focusing; concentrating; self-calming; and celebrating. Whilst the division of topics in this way will aid the process of evaluating and adapting ideas to suit specific needs, many of the games and activities could in fact be placed in more than one section, and I would urge you not to feel restricted by this division in choosing appropriate activities once you have become familiar with the general format.

Part Two includes a selection of activities based on well-known mindfulness meditation exercises, but the book is not by any means a course in meditation for children (there are many excellent books which focus solely on this area[1]). The mindfulness of Mindfulness Play is also not an approach to academic learning or a way of 'doing something' with children that will teach them how to be calm and attentive. It is a way of 'being' for both adults and children that extends into all the games and activities and ultimately into everyday life. I would, therefore, strongly recommend that you try out the 'Body focus' exercise on p.96 and the 'Mindfulness of breathing' activity on p.121 before using the games and activities in this book with children. This will give you a heightened awareness of how it is possible to develop mindfulness during simple focusing activities.[2]

I am only too aware of how little time most of us have in our busy lives to read about theory and its relevance to our work or to everyday interactions with our own children, and yet this is such a vital starting point. I am certain that using the ideas in Part Two of this book without putting them into the context of any theory at all would still have some beneficial outcomes for some children, particularly those who are already developing a healthy degree of emotional resilience and insight. But I am even more certain that it is possible to create negative outcomes by embarking on games and activities from an erroneous perspective (e.g. 'This game will teach children how to increase their attention span'). Some of the theory may already be familiar to you or you may feel that certain chapters are more useful for your particular needs than others. Whichever way you choose to use the material, my hope is that it will both confirm to you what you already know and that it will encourage you to meet more and more children in the wonderfully magic territory between our two worlds, carrying a few extra tools in your toolbox.

---

1   See, for example, *Teaching Children to Meditate* by David Fontana and Ingrid Slack (2007). Fontana and Slack are psychologists who have extensive experience of meditation and child psychology.

2   For further exploration of mindfulness in everyday life I recommend Charles Tart's book 'Living the Mindful Life'

How the games and activities are structured

Each game/activity has been marked with a set of symbols to aid in the selection of the most appropriate ones for different groups of children:

⑤	This gives an indication of the suggested *youngest* age for playing the basic game (unadapted). No upper age limit is given.
⏲ 10 minutes	An approximate time is suggested for the length of the game (excluding the discussion time). This will, of course, vary according to the size of the group and the ability of the players.
♦ ♦ ♦	Indicates that the game is suitable for larger groups (eight or more).
♦ ♦	The game is suitable for small groups.
♡♡♡	The game involves a lot of speaking unless it is adapted.
♡♡	A moderate amount of speaking is required by players.
♡	The game is primarily a non-verbal game or one requiring minimal speech.
☑ self-awareness (E)	This gives an indication of a foundation element (E), ability (A) or specific skill (S) used or developed by playing this game.

For each activity I have given one suggestion for foundation elements, abilities and specific skills that might be targeted during different games and activities, but the potential usage is, of course, much greater (see Chapters 5 and 6 for further explanations of *elements*, *abilities* and *skills*). There is therefore space for you to add other possibilities relevant to your own focus of work. By familiarising yourself with this framework, the interplay of the levels will soon become apparent and, undoubtedly, the more often that you engage in each activity, the more you will want to add to the lists.

Adaptations

Ideas for adaptations are offered as a spur to encourage you to be imaginatively creative in a way that suits your personal style and the developmental levels and learning needs of the children with whom you work. The ways in which the games are adapted and incorporated into family life and into educational and therapy approaches can and should vary according to the setting and according to the needs, strengths and experiences of the children. Each adult who facilitates games will naturally bring his or her own personality, imagination, expertise and knowledge to the games and create something new from the basic format. Also, because of the nature of group dynamics, the same game played with a different group will inevitably have a different feel to it and probably have different outcomes for the participants. In this way, playing with the process of playing becomes an integral part of our own learning.

In my own work, some spontaneous adaptations of activities have occurred when I have made a mistake and the children have laughed at the absurdities that have resulted. Although my mistakes were not originally deliberate, I soon realised the importance of tapping into a child's ability to understand and tolerate ambiguity and contradiction – an important aspect of creative thinking. Sharing moments of laughter, problem solving and creativity during games can be rewarding and reaffirming for everyone concerned.

I have also found Bob Eberle's work (e.g. Eberle 2008) in relation to creative ideas to be a useful tool when thinking about how to adapt activities to suit children at different ages and stages and how to create new games.

Based on original ideas by Alex Osborn (1953), Eberle uses SCAMPER as an acronym for strategies that can be used to make changes to existing ideas: Substitute, Combine, Adapt, Modify, Put to another use, Eliminate, Reverse. SCAMPER can be used to formulate questions you might ask yourself in relation to the games and activities presented in Part Two.

1. *Substitute.* Explore what might happen if you substitute one element for another. Can the game be played with different equipment? Can the rules of the game be changed? What happens if you change one part of the game? What if you played it in a different place and with different-sized groups? What if two children were leaders together?

2. *Combine.* What happens if you combine elements? What materials could be combined? Can you combine elements of two different games to make a third option? Can you bring two different groups of children together?

3. *Adapt.* How can you adjust a game/activity to suit different levels of ability/learning styles? Do you know of another game/activity that has similar learning aims? Can you adjust the discussions after the game to suit particular topics?

4. *Modify.* What can be modified, magnified or minified? Can you change the colours, shapes, number, size of the equipment being used? Can you increase/decrease the number of turns that each leader has?

5. *Put to another use.* What can you use this game for, other than its most obvious use?

6. *Eliminate.* What can you get rid of? What part of the game isn't needed for this group/child/learning situation?

7. *Reverse.* What can you reverse or rearrange? What if you changed the order of what you do? What if you look at this from the perspective of a different child or group? What if you let the child/children lead a whole session?

Expansion ideas

An important aspect of Mindfulness Play is the opportunity that this gives for children to expand their thinking skills and their imagination and to learn to trust their instincts. When given the freedom to verbalise some of their intuitive feelings and thoughts, children will often surprise us with remarkable insights.

To aid this process, each game/activity is followed by suggestions for further reflection and discussion. You will find that many of the expansion ideas given for each game will be relevant for other games too. As a general principle, I would suggest that we should not give more time to a discussion at the time of playing than we do to the game itself. Many children who play games regularly gain insights into their own thoughts, behaviour and emotions and those of others purely through the experience, and will not necessarily need to take specific time in every session to reflect on what happened. However, these topics do also provide an opportunity for drawing links between different themes at later times. You could remind children of particular games when this is relevant: 'Do you remember when we played that game of... What did you find out about listening?' or 'How might this game help us to understand what happened in the class yesterday?' Even the briefest time spent in thinking about how the games relate to specific aspects of focusing, concentrating and calming within a child's everyday experiences can help him to make enormous leaps in realisation.

Each game description also includes space for you to add your own notes. These might include such things as personal perceptions and experiences of using the games, personal preferences, dislikes, problems and successes, and any issues raised concerning age, cultural or gender differences.

Additional notes and reflections

Finally, because you will undoubtedly have many more games and activities in your repertoire and will gather extra ideas from colleagues and children, each of the games sections ends with a blank summary page for additional notes.

Here you can add to your list and make any further general comments on your experiences with the games that you have used.

My hope is that this format will encourage reflective practice but that it will not *dis*courage enjoying the pure fun of playing games with young children. This, after all, is one of the essential values of Mindfulness Play – having fun while learning about ourselves and others!

Further guidelines for facilitating Mindfulness Play can be found in Chapters 3 and 4.

2

Understanding Attention and Concentration

Key concepts

- Attending and concentrating are a natural part of our lives.

- A child's capacity to control the focus of her attention is dependent on developmental and environmental factors.

- Developing strategies for self-calming, focusing and concentrating will lead to long-lasting benefits for well-being.

Attending and concentrating are a natural part of our lives

Each of us selectively attends to different stimuli throughout the day, shifting our awareness from external experiences to internal thoughts and feelings, and changing our level of engagement with these different aspects of our world according to our personal abilities, needs and preferences, our motivation to attend or the intensity of the stimulus. These processes are a natural part of our lives, and ones we can easily take for granted because they are often largely subconscious. Even while reading this page you will perhaps have switched from focusing on the written words to an internal thought and will have simultaneously filtered out extraneous stimuli such as a clock ticking in the room or the sound of traffic outside (and, in reading that, you may well have suddenly noticed these noises!).

Redirecting our attention can also be made much more conscious. We can choose *where* to direct our awareness and we can learn *how* to direct it. When we know how to direct our attention effectively we can, for example, notice and then change an unwanted internal stimulus (e.g. unnecessary muscle tension or a thought that is causing us to feel anxious); we can notice and value intuitive feelings and ideas; we can filter out unnecessary stimuli that might interfere with concentration on a task; and we can notice the smallest of details in our environment or choose to take a wider view. In so doing, we are basically choosing to give emphasis to different areas of our experience. We are not denying or belittling the existence of other dimensions of that experience, simply deciding to put our focus and energies into one aspect.

There are, of course, some children for whom attention control is a specific difficulty – for example, children with attention deficit hyperactivity disorder (ADHD) – and others for whom sustaining joint attention with another person may be a particular problem – for example, some children with autism. Joint attention involves coordinating your interest in an object or event with someone else's interest in the same object or event. This is a tricky process, requiring not only the capacity to attend but also the capacity to understand and use a number of different social skills.

Deciding where to focus attention and knowing how to do this are vital components of well-being. The ability to maintain this focus, through a degree of self-awareness and self-control, leads to concentration, and effective concentration contributes to perseverance. When we concentrate, we put energy into action, or, as the philosopher Keyserling said:

> The ability to concentrate is a real propelling power of the totality of our psychic mechanism. Nothing elevates our capacity of action more than its development. Any success, no matter in which area, can be explained by the intelligent use of this capacity. (Keyserling quoted in Ferrucci 1982, p.30)

Children who have problems with this area of development may be further at risk because inevitably, they are more likely to experience difficulties in building and maintaining effective social interactions with other children and with adults. Understanding the ways in which these abilities develop can give us some insight into how we might help children to build or regain them and therefore enhance well-being.

A child's capacity to control the focus of her attention is
dependent on developmental and environmental factors

Even very young children have the aptitude to engage for inordinate lengths of time in something that they are enjoying, especially if it does not require complex thought processes (I remember playing 'I'm the lion eating my food' with my two-year-old niece for a good ten minutes!). It would seem that young children do not necessarily have difficulty in attending and concentrating per se but rather in consciously controlling the *focus* of their attention, particularly when they are being asked to focus on something that is adult-directed (and therefore not of their own choosing). This is a complex process: children need to be able to control initial arousal or awareness of that object or event, sustain their alertness and continue to be selectively attentive, recognising and filtering out unnecessary distractions. They also need to learn when such coordination is necessary (Samuels and Edwall 1981). Learning this conscious control is partly dependent on the inbuilt temperament of the child and partly dependent on a number of different cognitive processes such as memory and flexibility of thought.

When we have been attending to something for a sustained period of time (perhaps a difficult puzzle, a new skill, a complex problem-solving activity) or we have focused intensively on inhibiting unwanted stimuli, thoughts or impulses, we appear to reach a maximum capacity point, known as attention fatigue (see Box 2.1). In effect, the mechanism for attention control ceases to function efficiently for periods of time, making it more and more difficult to pay attention and also more difficult to inhibit impulsivity. This is a phenomenon apparent in very young infants too. Sustained attention in infants is evident but is usually episodic, and it has been suggested that infants may need space between periods of active focus in order to process the information gathered and to self-regulate (Parrinello and Ruff 1988). As I'm sure many of us have seen, some infants when over-stimulated for too long without pauses may start to cry or show other signs of distress.

Perhaps under such conditions of overload, older children might conceivably view the act of focusing attention to be hard work and stressful. If this is the case, then this could, in turn, trigger the release of stress hormones, fuelling the body for a flight or fight reaction. The consequences of this might also be very familiar to many of us – when children have reached such a saturation point, they can quickly start to feel frustrated, anxious, grumpy or downright aggressive!

Box 2.1 Attention control and the brain

It appears that different aspects of attention also involve distinct areas of the brain. The parietal lobe, for example, is active in selective attention (focusing on specific aspects of the environment) and in shifting attention from one aspect to another. This information is then passed to the cingulate gyrus (which stretches from the front to the back of the brain) and to the frontal lobes. The cingulate gyrus is responsible for filtering out irrelevant information (selective attention) and for sustaining attention on one stimulus over another. The frontal lobes are vital to the formation of our personality and perform many different functions. With regard to attention, they perform a supervisory role. For example, they enable flexible thinking and the ability to focus on more than one task at the same time (Nunn, Hanstock and Lask 2008).

There is emerging evidence that problems with joint attention could be partly linked with variability in the functioning of the ventromedial prefrontal cortex (Dawson *et al.* 2002). The prefrontal cortex, as its name suggests, constitutes the front part of the frontal lobes. Without a well-developed prefrontal cortex, children will have difficulty not only with self-control and self-regulation but also with the ability to feel 'connected' to others. The right prefrontal cortex plays a vital part in our capacity to deliberately direct our attention. It is also associated with the phenomenon of 'attention fatigue' (Glosser and Goodglass 1990). Regular 'insight' or mindfulness meditation practised over a prolonged period of time appears to have a physiological effect on this region, resulting in a thickening of the cortex and possibly leading to enhanced sensory, cognitive and emotional processing (Lazar *et al.* 2005).

With increasing age, however, children do appear to develop a variety of attention strategies. They learn how to cope with distractions and to switch their attention successfully and appropriately from one stimulus to another in the presence of these distractions, so that by about 11–12 years of age most children are able to successfully focus on material that is relevant to a particular task and ignore irrelevant material. In fact, one study has shown that extraneous stimuli (in this case, playing children's music in the background while children performed visual discrimination tasks), although impairing the concentration of younger children, can actually facilitate concentration in older children because they appear to actively adapt to the distractions and focus more intently on the task (Higgins and Turnure 1984). This is, of course, dependent on how difficult the task is and on the type and intensity of distraction (even older children will tend to have more difficulty in sustaining their concentration when background distractions are intermittent or varied) but, most importantly, it is highly dependent on the *motivation* of the child to attend (see Chapter 4).

So – I have walked into a busy classroom and wondered how any child could possibly concentrate on their individual or small group tasks with such constant noise going on, yet they do. I imagine that all of us have had experience of 'adapting' to constant background noise (such as music) and even sometimes finding it a comfort and an aid to concentration, missing it when it stops. Equally, you may have experienced times when intermittent and varied noise, such as someone doing a bit of DIY in the room next door, has had a negative effect on your ability to concentrate. And if you are trying to focus on something that doesn't particularly interest you, but which you are required to do, then unwanted noise, people coming and going around you, whispering (as in a library where students are trying to work) and so on can be particularly problematic.

Developing strategies for self-calming, focusing and concentrating will lead to long-lasting benefits for well-being

Although such capacities take time to develop, there is increasing evidence that introducing children as young as four or five to specific strategies for self-calming, focusing and concentrating can have long-lasting benefits.

We know, for example, that regular use of some forms of meditative practice, involving focusing attention on one particular stimulus such as a sound or word(s) (mantra), a visual stimulus such as a mandala or a candle flame or a physical stimulus such as awareness of your own breath can have positive benefits for people experiencing mental health difficulties and can enhance pain control (Kabat-Zinn 1996).[1] The effective use of meditation causes the body to release natural opioids into the bloodstream, resulting in the subjective experience of feeling calm. Already, in some schools in the UK and USA, starting lessons with a brief silent meditation is a natural part of the day, or children may focus their attention by practising tai chi or yoga or some form of more vigorous physical exercise. As a regular practice, this enables children to learn how to control the focus of their attention and also how to relax themselves in body and mind. In other words, attention is not focused in an intense 'hard work' sort of way but rather in a 'being in the moment' way – really noticing body, thoughts and feelings and aiming to bring the focus of attention into just one area.

Importantly, the relationship between being physically and mentally calm and relaxed and being able to focus and concentrate works both ways. So we

---

1   Jon Kabat-Zinn's book *Full Catastrophe Living: How to Cope with Stress, Pain and Illness Using Mindfulness Meditation* is particularly useful in exploring this aspect.

know, for example, that children who take part in a period of mindfulness training often show improvements in attention strategies and decreased impulsivity, whilst children who take part in regular peer massage are also reported to be 'less fidgety' and more able to concentrate on their subsequent lessons. The Massage in Schools Programme, developed by Mia Elmsäter from Sweden and Sylvie Hétu from Canada, is now being used in many UK schools as a way of helping children to build self-esteem and respect for each other. Positive touch, such as this type of massage (performed by children on each other and given on the back, head, arms and neck only), releases oxytocin in the brain. This is the hormone known to aid the 'bonding' process after childbirth and it is associated with the regulation of the stress hormone, cortisol. Oxytocin has a calming and relaxing effect. Reports from teachers indicate that, among the many benefits of incorporating this programme into the curriculum, children are showing increased concentration levels, decreased levels of agitation and aggression, and are learning skills of empathy and tolerance.[2]

Recent research in the USA (Kuo and Faber Taylor 2004) has highlighted the benefits to children of spending time exposed to nature in terms of enhanced attention and reduced impulsivity. It has been suggested that spending regular periods of time in outdoor green spaces is particularly conducive to helping children with ADHD to focus and concentrate and that this could be partly due to the natural 'restorative effect' of engaging the mind effortlessly (Kaplan 1995).

Some of the games and activities in this book are designed to enhance children's capacity to use their imaginations effectively. Effective imagination, as already noted, is one of the core abilities for well-being. The mind and the body are in constant communication with each other as different systems of the body respond to messages from the mind and vice versa. Images play an important role in this communication. For example, the imagination directly affects the autonomic nervous system (ANS) – that part of our nervous system which controls such things as heart rate, breathing, circulation, body temperature and digestive processes. The ANS helps to maintain the constancy of our internal environment (homeostasis). How can the imagination affect this complex system? If I tell myself to increase my heart rate or to sweat, I'm not likely to notice much response, but if I imagine a frightening experience vividly enough, then my body will respond as if it is actually happening.

---

2   'Touch therapies' have also been successful in helping some children with autism to stay on task for increased periods of time and have been linked to autistic children showing increased social relatedness in the classroom (Field *et al.* 1996).

Working on this principle, various studies have highlighted the possibility of using images to effect *positive* changes in the body. Dr Karen Olness, Professor of Paediatrics, Family Medicine, and International Health at Case Western Reserve University, Ohio, has demonstrated how image messages can have an effect in the treatment of migraines. She has shown that children who regularly practise a relaxation imagery exercise have far fewer migraines than children taking conventional medicine for the same reason. Olness, who uses biofeedback systems to show children how 'thinking' can affect their body, feels that it would benefit every child, beginning at age six or seven, to have an opportunity to be hooked up to a biofeedback system in order to experience the realisation: 'change my thinking and my body changes' (Olness 1993).

Imagination is an ability that acts at many levels. We can harness the imagination to deliberately aid concentration as in the use of guided visualisations. We can imagine objects, sounds and smells and focus our attention on these internally without the actual object, sound or smell being in our presence. We can recall images, mantras, colours and so on to focus our attention away from the ceaseless chatter of our minds. We can heighten the focus of our attention on another person by imagining what it might be like for her to be who she is (empathy) and so move our attention away from our own concerns and troubles when appropriate. We can also make use of personal imagery to help us to tap into our natural creativity and intuitive awareness of ourselves and others (Plummer 2007a).

Making such powerful tools more accessible to children carries a weighty responsibility. Mindfulness Play offers a vehicle for doing just this.

3

Mindfulness Play

Key concepts

- Mindfulness Play involves 'awakened' interactions.

- Learning through play is a natural part of a child's development.

- Games:

  o provide structure and predictability

  o reflect aspects of real life

  o provide valuable opportunities for growth and learning.

- Mindfulness Play is a way of being.

Mindfulness Play involves 'awakened' interactions

Some years ago I was walking along a beach, admiring and collecting small pebbles of many different shapes and colours. An unusual number of these were almost perfectly flat circles. As I picked up each one and held it in my hand, I was struck by the thought that although some of the stones had not yet been worn into circles, given the right environmental conditions they certainly had the potential to be further smoothed and shaped. I had an image of each individual's unique potential as a bag of these pebbles – a bagful of perfect possibilities.

Nurturing a child's possibilities involves 'taking care' at many levels. Watching out for a child's well-being, whilst still allowing them the chance to build resilience and *self*-nurturing skills, requires a delicate balance between supporting and letting go. Children will, of course, build and develop social, emotional and spiritual well-being through coping with trials and setbacks as well as through triumphs.

As already suggested in Chapter 1, I believe we can be most effective in achieving this balance if we are able to nurture our own awareness too. In essence, this involves developing a heightened degree of mindfulness – an awareness of ourselves, our emotions, actions and thoughts and the effects that we have on others – and an awareness of the child's point of view – his emotions, learning processes, strengths and challenges. This degree of awareness requires the capacity to develop our own skills of focusing attention, concentrating and self-calming.

Charles Tart's description of mindfulness as 'perceptual intelligence' is very relevant to my own concept of Mindfulness Play. Tart makes a clear distinction between consideration of others shown through conditioning or 'habit' and the more awakened ability to 'see more accurately and discriminatingly and so behave more appropriately toward others and toward our inner selves...' (Tart 1994, p.6). The idea of mindfulness as a form of intelligence, rather like emotional intelligence, is appealing because it suggests that we can develop and nurture mindfulness toward others and mindfulness toward ourselves and that we can help children to nurture this 'way of being' – giving added weight to the importance of attending, concentrating and self-calming. If we can do this through play, then all the better.

David Cohen famously exclaimed, 'Ponder the irony! Children are the experts at play, play is their work and yet we, long-out-of-practice oldies, think we can teach them how to play!' (Cohen 1993, p.13). But Vivian Paley's expansion on this perhaps more closely fits with the main concept of Mindfulness Play: 'We were taught to say that play is the work of children. But watching and listening to them, I saw that play was nothing less than Truth and Life' (1991, p.17).

As a nursery teacher, Paley became increasingly aware of how children in her classes placed a great deal of emphasis on things that happened during play activities – it was the themes that arose during play that they were most likely to want to discuss. In her wonderful book *The Boy Who Would Be a Helicopter*, Paley observes that children's rites and images in play:

> seem mainly concerned with the uses of friendship and fantasy to avoid
> fear and loneliness and to establish a comfortable relationship with people

and events. In play, the child says, 'I can *do* this well; I can *be* this effectively; I *understand* what is happening to me and to other children.' (Paley 1991, p.10)

Mindfulness Play involves understanding and respecting children's 'rites' and 'images'.

Learning through play is a natural part of a child's development

The universality of play and traditional games highlights the importance of this aspect of children's development and well-being. From early babyhood, through our childhood years and often into adulthood (through sports activities for example) play is how we find out about ourselves and the world. This process begins through manipulation of our own body (e.g. sucking a thumb or toes), play with sounds (babbling), play with objects (e.g. a comfort blanket or a soft toy) and play with significant people in our lives (e.g. the 'mirroring' of facial expression and body movements that often occurs so naturally between a parent and child, games of peek-a-boo and waving 'bye bye'). In this way, we gradually learn what is 'me' and 'not me' and we learn the rudiments of cause and effect and turn-taking. We even learn to cope with feelings of temporary separation and loss with games such as hide-and-seek and peek-a-boo.

From this type of play we move on gradually to symbolic play – manipulation of objects as symbols of real things – and then to imaginary play where some props may be used but much, or all, of the scenario is imagined. This type of engagement in the world of imagination gradually moves from solitary or parallel play to engagement in play with others: 'I'm the Mummy and I have to feed the baby', 'I will be the princess and you can be the wicked witch' or 'I'm a policeman and I'm looking for a robber.'

By working our imagination like a muscle, we learn to problem-solve, to tolerate frustration, to work through some of life's difficulties and so reach our own 'child-level' of understanding of the complexities of the world – we make 'child-sense' of our experiences in a simplified and safe way and thereby strengthen our emotional resilience.

Play of one sort or another provides invaluable opportunities for children to learn through imitation, to experience the consequences of their actions and to experiment with different skills and different outcomes without fear of failure or being judged unfavourably by others. It is also through play that children can expand and consolidate their language skills.

Psychologist Catherine Garvey suggests that:

because playing is voluntarily controlled (executed in a way in which imperfect achievement is minimally dangerous), its effects are probably intricately related to the child's mastery and integration of his experiences… when the behaviour is next performed in a non-play mode, it may be more skilled, better integrated, and associated with a richer or wider range of meaning. In this way play can contribute to the expertise of the player and to his effectiveness in the non-play world. (Garvey 1977, p.118)

Play during childhood can encourage a 'playful' approach to life at a later age, including the ability to bring humour and fun to relationships and to see life's difficulties as challenges rather than insurmountable obstacles. It helps children to develop social awareness and conscience and creates opportunities to explore concepts of fairness and equality.

We now know that pleasurable, playful experiences affect the chemical balance and neurological make-up of the brain. For example, imaginative and creative play is known to lower levels of stress chemicals, enabling children to deal more successfully with stressful situations. Gentle rough-and-tumble play and laughter are also known to have anti-stress effects, activating the brain's emotion-regulating centres and causing the release of opioids, the natural brain chemicals that induce feelings of pleasure and well-being (Sunderland 2007).

The relaxation and restorative effects of engaging the mind effortlessly (see Chapter 2), as in some forms of play, are well known. Alternating between focused concentration and engaging the mind effortlessly is also a key component in moments of inspiration. You might concentrate on solving a problem and get absolutely nowhere (or so you think); then you go for a walk or soak in a bath or begin to drift into sleep and suddenly the answer comes. This moment of insight comes not from relaxation alone but from the combination of concerted effort *followed* by a period of relaxation. This is an important concept in terms of Mindfulness Play: we facilitate children's engagement with games and activities that will promote relaxation and enjoyment, at the same time helping them to become more self-aware and promoting core abilities and specific skills needed for well-being.

Play is undoubtedly fun, and having fun is good for us! Mindfulness Play contributes to a child's well-being in ways that transcend the actual activity itself. If a child is genuinely having fun and is sharing that enjoyment with others, then he is in effect celebrating life – he is engaging in the joy of living – and if, through facilitated games, he is also gaining new ideas and learning new skills, then we will know that we have succeeded in meeting him 'mindfully' and with respect in that shared space of insight between our adult and child worlds.

Games provide structure and predictability

How do games fit into this magical world of play? Garvey defines games as play activities that are structured with 'explicit rules that can be precisely communicated' (1977, p.101).

The ability to play games with rules usually emerges at around five or six years of age, although, as outlined above, the early signs of this can be seen with very young infants (a game of peek-a-boo, for example, involves structured turn-taking to some extent, and children of three often understand the 'unspoken' rules of familiar games). By around five years of age, children are more able to tolerate waiting and a degree of inevitable frustration at being 'out' in a competitive game. They are beginning to exercise self-control and are developing the ability to follow rules and conventions. They are also more able to sustain interactions with others for longer periods.

Games generally have clear start and finishing points and follow sequences that are accepted by the players and which can therefore be replicated at other times and in different situations. These 'process' rules provide a sense of predictability and security, even when the game itself might be a bit scary, and in this way various real life issues that might be too difficult or painful to confront head-on can be played out in safety. Such games may perhaps even engender laughter and enjoyment whilst nevertheless dealing with important life issues.

Opie and Opie conducted extensive research into children's street games in the 1960s. They observed that:

> Children like games in which there is a sizeable element of luck, so that individual abilities cannot be directly compared. They like games which restart almost automatically, so that everybody is given a new chance. They like games which move in stages, in which each stage, the choosing of leaders, the picking-up of sides, the determining of which child shall start, is almost a game in itself...many of the games, particularly those of young children, are more akin to ceremonies than competitions. In these games children gain the reassurance that comes with repetition, and the feeling of fellowship that comes from doing the same as everyone else. (Opie and Opie 1976, pp.394–5)

Some childhood games are culturally specific whereas others can be found in various forms across different cultures.[1] Interestingly, a study carried out by Roberts and Sutton-Smith in 1962 found evidence of an association between

---

1   See, for example, *Let's Play Asian Children's Games* (Dunn 1978) published by the Asian Cultural Centre for UNESCO.

the type of games played (whether they were predominantly based on strategy, skill or luck) and the type of upbringing of different groups of children (where the emphasis was placed on responsibility, achievement or obedience). Whatever the main orientation of games might be, however, they all provide children with the opportunity to explore the function of rules and conventions and to safely test the boundaries of what is acceptable to others within a fun and rewarding but nevertheless rule-governed activity.

In games, children who have difficulty in understanding and expressing their feelings verbally can begin to explore difficult emotions in safety and with the spirit of 'play'. In this way, games help in the process of reflection and demonstrate to children that they are not alone in their feelings and that others have things in common with them. This aspect of games can easily be enhanced through careful facilitation by an adult.

Mindfulness Play is a way of being

For me, one of the joys of using familiar, structured games and activities has been the realisation of the richness of learning that occurs through engaging creatively with the simplest of ideas.

This being said, I am sure that each of us has had experience of being involved in games and activities that just didn't seem to work, even though they had been carefully chosen to suit the needs of particular children. Picture the following imaginary scenario:

> Seven-year-old Adam is joining in with a group game of 'By the Sea' – an active, fun game chosen by group facilitator Maggie to help the children to let off steam. The group has previously been concentrating on a written task which proved quite difficult for Adam. You're already OUT, Adam! comes the indignant cry from Ben. 'You can't keep joining in when you're ALREADY OUT!' Maggie invites Adam to stand near her and help her to decide who is out next time. Adam reluctantly agrees but during the next round insists that Ben is 'out'. The game quickly deteriorates into a series of denials and second chances. Finally, an exhausted Maggie brings things to an early close when she spots Adam systematically emptying out the contents of the sand tray in the far corner of the room. (*Self-Esteem Games for Children*, Plummer 2007b, p.7)

Why is it that some games seem to work well with one group and not with another? I believe that one of the main reasons lies in how well the person who is facilitating the games understands the importance of the game process and how powerful this process can be. Of course, games played as energisers or treats can be exciting and fun and a source of immense pleasure for the players.

Occasionally, however, they can also be sheer torture for the quiet child, the child who has difficulty in understanding the rules of games, the child who is already full of pent-up frustration or anxiety or the child who fears being 'left out' or losing yet again.

In contrast, a well-chosen game played with awareness on the part of the facilitator can be an incredibly effective instrument for supporting a child's emergent sense of self and for helping him to tolerate frustration and learn to cooperate with his peers.

Of course, there is no single method or game that can be guaranteed to appeal to all children or consistently help to solve particular problems or ensure certain responses. However, games are undoubtedly an important part of a child's development. Without this awareness on our part, the many opportunities for helping children to build and maintain physical, cognitive, social and emotional well-being through the medium of games can so easily be missed, or, worse still, we may unwittingly foster feelings of low self-esteem in children and trigger uncomfortably intense or inappropriate emotional responses.

Our interactions with children, in whatever capacity, should always be based on our knowledge and understanding of them as individuals. It is by listening to what children are telling us and by walking alongside them on their journey of self-discovery and mastery that we can learn most about how they view the world and themselves, and therefore how best to support them.

As mindful facilitators of the game process, we can make certain hypotheses about the ways in which children participate in structured games. First, the way a child acts and reacts in a game situation is likely to reflect his life experiences in some way and therefore also reflect how he behaves in other situations. So, without being overly analytical or too literal in our interpretations of children's behaviour during play, it is nevertheless important for us to be aware of general patterns. Are there children who take a long time to warm up to each activity? Are there some who are taking over? What happens when children become frustrated or cannot tolerate waiting their turn? Are they able to recognise personal achievements and those of others? Do they behave independently or always look to others to take the lead? Are they able to take on different roles at different times or for different types of game?

A second hypothesis that we might make centres on children's capacity for change. Working within a humanistic framework, we can approach the playing of games and participation in group activities with the assumption that all children, whatever their current abilities, have within them the resources, and therefore the potential, for change and growth. However small or large the changes might be, the ability to respond with a degree of flexibility in different situations and the ability to learn from active participation is part of what it is to be human.

Finally, we should also remember that each child's attitude to different games, his degree of participation and his enjoyment of the game will change over time as he matures and learns.

This mindful awareness of children is naturally facilitated by engaging in our own reflections about the games and processes too. As an aid to my own reflective practice, these are some of the questions that I have found helpful when planning and reviewing sessions. You might find it helpful to consider gradually incorporating some of these into your own practice over time:

- What is my role as the facilitator?

- How will I set the tone of the session/introduce the activities in a fun way?

- Why are we playing these particular games? What are my aims/ intended outcomes?

- How will I know if I've achieved my aims/outcomes?

- What are my personal feelings about these activities? If I was this child's age, would I enjoy playing these games?

- Are the activities appropriate for the age/cultural background of the child/children in the group?

- Do I know the 'rules' of the games?

- Who (if anyone) in the group will find the activities difficult/ challenging/easy?

- Do I need to adapt the activities in any way to allow/encourage full participation of all group members?

- What back-up strategies will I need?

- How will I handle behaviour that is potentially disruptive to the group?

- Am I aware of why this behaviour might occur?

- If the group is large or diverse in needs, do I have a 'support' person available?

- What will I do if a child knows a different version of a game and wants to play that? (You might suggest that you play their version next time, or it might be appropriate to share different versions at the time and abandon one of the other games you had planned.)

- Is this the right time for the game/activity?

- Is the room the right temperature?

- Am I feeling up to it?

After completion of a session it is useful to take a few moments as soon as possible to reflect on the activities:

- What went well?

- Was there anything that was difficult to monitor?

- What skills did you use?

- What did you enjoy about the activities?

- What did the children most enjoy?

- Was each activity of an appropriate length?

- Was the level right for the child/whole group?

- Did you introduce and summarise activities effectively?

- Did you achieve your objectives?

- If you were to do a similar session again, would you change it in any way? Why?

- What would you do differently?

- How would you extend/alter each activity to move the child/group on to the next stage when they are ready?

- Were there any issues raised concerning age, cultural or gender differences which will need to be addressed?

Mindfulness Play is facilitated by careful structuring of the emotional environment. This aspect is explored in the following chapter.

4

Structuring the Emotional Environment for Mindfulness Play

Key concepts

- Mindfulness Play involves creating a nurturing environment.

- Roles, rules and boundaries need to be clearly defined so that children feel safe.

- A nurturing environment is one in which all emotions are acknowledged and valued.

- Nurturing environments encourage motivation to focus, concentrate and self-calm.

Mindfulness Play involves creating a nurturing environment

Mindfulness Play involves careful consideration of the emotional environment in order to promote an appropriate emotional and mindful state in children and thus facilitate their well-being. In practical terms, we can achieve this through consideration of three key areas:

1. establishing roles, rules and boundaries

2. understanding and valuing emotions

3. supporting motivation to focus, concentrate and self-calm.

The next section looks at each of these areas in turn and explores them in relation to playing games in groups. However, although the focus is on group interactions, the principles apply just as much to playing games with individual children or within families.

Roles, rules and boundaries need to be clearly defined so that children feel safe

For some children, new games can be scary and we need to spend time building trust among group members and between ourselves and the children we are supporting. Trust is most easily maintained if roles, rules and boundaries are clearly established at the start of a group. This can help children to feel 'contained' and safe, which in turn will allow them to engage in play more fully.

ROLES

Because of the multifaceted nature of games, there will be multiple roles for those who choose to coordinate games sessions with young children. Although these may change and evolve over time, being clear about which role(s) you are taking on will help children to understand their own roles and boundaries and will help you to structure and reflect on the sessions more effectively. Possible roles might include several of the following at any one time:

- role model

- teacher/provider of challenges

- facilitator/encourager/enabler

- supporter/helper

- mediator/arbitrator

- observer

- participant

- researcher/information gatherer/assessor

- supervisor

- provider of fun

- ideas person

- timekeeper.

Consider whether or not the roles you are taking on conflict in any way and, if so, which one you most want to concentrate on. Perhaps a second person is needed to take a different perspective or role? For example, can you be facilitator/encourager and also record information about how individuals are coping with different aspects of a particular game?

In which role are you happiest? Do you feel most comfortable as 'provider of fun' or most comfortable in the 'teaching' role?

What about the roles of the children? These too may change and evolve over time so that group members each have the opportunity to be the game coordinator, the 'ideas person' or the 'teacher'. Those who feel unable to join in with a particular game may enjoy being timekeeper or observer. Children who understand the rules of games and can explain these to others may naturally take on the role of arbitrator or game coordinator, leading others in making choices and in ensuring that the rules are understood and followed by all participants. This is a valuable skill that can be facilitated during many of the games suggested in this book.

Monitoring of games by the participants themselves is an important aspect of Mindfulness Play. Children who would normally find this role difficult can be gradually encouraged and supported in leading and monitoring fairly. Those children who have plenty of experience in arbitrating and leading games can also be encouraged to support this process by stepping back to allow others to have a go.

RULES

In their daily lives, children have to negotiate their way through a welter of adult-imposed rules, structures and boundaries. Sometimes these are explicit, but often they are unclear or unspoken, taken for granted by the adults but a potential minefield for children who forget, don't know or don't understand them. Constant insistence on adherence to adult-imposed rules in games may similarly have a negative effect on the process, resulting in children disengaging with the games, rebelling or becoming passive. Rules should therefore be flexible enough to accommodate different types or levels of response.

A major way in which children will learn to understand and respect rules is by having experience of devising them for themselves, preferably by negotiating with others, and then trying them out. In this way, they learn that games are usually only successful when everyone adheres to the rules but that there can also be differing versions and perspectives. They learn that they have choices and that others will listen to their ideas.

Older children can also be given plenty of opportunities to invent new versions of familiar games and to alter the rules of games in discussion with other group members. Experimentation with the structure of games helps children to understand the value of rules and to distinguish more easily between what works and what doesn't. Discussion with peers also provides opportunities for developing skills in negotiating and decision making. Before any alterations are made, it is, of course, important to make it clear to all players that there are certain safety and non-discriminatory rules which must always be followed.

Games sessions also need 'rules' or guidelines to help foster the feeling of trust and safety among those taking part and to help ensure that the group is a safe place to be. Two of the most important rules for facilitators to make clear are:

1. *Children will always be given the choice of staying in or out of the game.*
    For children who opt out frequently you may want to suggest
    an alternative role such as timekeeper to encourage some initial
    involvement. For some anxious children, observing others engaging
    in a game without feeling in any way included could allow the
    build-up of negative emotions, whereas for others it gives them
    the opportunity to prepare themselves to join in by watching what
    happens and familiarising themselves with the rules. We should also
    remember that each child's attitude to different activities, her degree
    of participation and her enjoyment of the activity will change over
    time as she matures and learns.

2. *Children who are reluctant to take part straight away may choose to join in at*
    any time by giving a signal. (Note: If the group appears generally restless,
    do not insist on continuing for a certain number of set rounds of a
    game; take it as an indication that it is not the right time to play this
    game or that it is not the right game for this group.)

Further guidelines should be established for the reflection/discussion time. In order for children to feel comfortable when contributing to these sessions, they need to know that their ideas and opinions are valued and that they will be listened to without judgement from others and without being interrupted. Individual differences in social customs, beliefs and behaviours should also be acknowledged and an atmosphere of open discussion should be encouraged. Children need to feel safe enough to be able to say what is the 'norm' for their family or culture when this differs from the general consensus of the group.

Older children can also be encouraged to explore differing opinions where appropriate, thus giving them the opportunity to debate a point constructively.

It is also the facilitator's task to demonstrate a firm but fair approach in order to prevent difficulties arising – for example, from children being consistently very dominant or ridiculed by others because they do not understand the game rules. It is crucial that all group members (including family groups) understand the importance of supporting each other's participation – even games that purport to be non-competitive can sometimes be played in a competitive, even aggressive way unless there are clear guidelines.

BOUNDARIES

An example of a clear time boundary might be:

> 'Today the games session will be ten minutes long and when we have finished the game we will do X.'

Or:

> 'Every morning we will play one game during circle time and then we will…'

The focus of each game should also be made explicit where appropriate. For example, you might introduce a warm-up game by telling the children that it is a game for getting to know each other better. Where you are intending to follow a game with a discussion about a specific ability or skill, you might set the focus with a more detailed introduction, perhaps by telling a short story or recounting a fictitious event to illustrate your point. You could then introduce the chosen game(s) as being a way of exploring that skill. As children become used to the format, they can be encouraged to choose familiar games (perhaps from a small selection of possible options) which they think might be relevant for a particular skill. This process of choosing can also engender useful discussions about how skills are learned and developed.

A nurturing environment is one in which all emotions are acknowledged and valued

Of course, no one can be 'calm' all the time, nor is it possible or desirable to focus our attention on the outside world for sustained periods without awareness of our inner thoughts and emotions. We therefore need to be aware of the many emotions that may be expressed during Mindfulness Play. Whilst these emotions may be directly related to the themes of play (in this instance, attending, concentrating and calming), there will certainly be others that arise simply because young children are naturally more inclined to live in the moment, to have thoughts and emotions about the emotions of other children in the group, to experience frustration in a game and so on. The games and activities in this book are all non-competitive where the enjoyment and the challenge come from the process itself rather than from winning. Competition against oneself can, of course, be very rewarding. Trying to beat your own best score is a common feature of many childhood games. However, although competitive activities can form an important part of a child's learning once she is ready to engage in them and does so by her own choice, the ability to cope successfully in competition with peers is a tricky hurdle to negotiate and one which will complicate the process of building other skills. Younger children and those who are particularly vulnerable to low self-esteem often find win-or-lose games extremely difficult to manage. For such children, the anticipation of the rewards of winning might be so great that the disappointment of losing has an equally dramatic effect on their mood. In order to enjoy and benefit from competitive games, they will therefore need to develop first a degree of emotional resilience, competence and self-efficacy, all of which can be fostered through non-competitive activities. The more that children engage in cooperative play, the more likely they are to understand how other children think and, undoubtedly, the more they will develop their capacity for emotionally (and perceptually) intelligent interactions.

When we acknowledge and validate a child's feelings we are effectively giving her the message that it is OK to have different emotions – it is OK to be upset, for example – and that we can have some control over the intensity of our emotions and learn how to control the behaviour that might result.

For example, if a child with a hearing difficulty says, 'I hate this game, it's stupid', then aiming to acknowledge and support rather than to rescue can help her to feel more in control. Responses such as 'But everyone else is enjoying it, I'm sure you will too', 'You haven't tried it yet, let's have a go together' or 'That's OK, you can sit this one out if you like', whilst well-meaning, do not help the child to understand her own feelings more fully or discover her own solutions in situations that she finds difficult.

Commenting on what you see, hear and feel and making a hypothesis about the feeling behind the words can help the child to feel understood and is more likely to lead to her making adjustments in her self-evaluation ('It's a very noisy game and I noticed that it's hard to hear the instructions sometimes. I wonder if it would be more fun for you to stand closer to the teacher').

Nurturing environments encourage motivation
to focus, concentrate and self-calm

Daniel Goleman (1996) refers to the ability to motivate ourselves as being an important aspect of emotional intelligence (see p.54). Motivation is, unfortunately, one of those nebulous concepts that is difficult to measure. But nonetheless we intrinsically know what it means to *feel* motivated and how much more exciting life is when we are motivated to learn new skills and develop our knowledge. It is undoubtedly the case that, although some children have a specific difficulty in focusing their attention and concentrating for any length of time (and there is obviously a developmental perspective to take into account), for many children, it is not the *inability* to pay attention to something that stops them from concentrating; it is the *motivation* to attend. A child will be more motivated to focus and concentrate if materials are relevant and manageable and if she feels engaged with the process (e.g. if she has helped to set her own targets or has contributed to the design of the activity or game). As psychologist David Wood exhorts us to remember:

> Attending, concentrating and memorizing are *activities*... Unless we embody the material to be learnt and remembered in a task that makes sense to the child, one that involves objectives he can realize and that draws his attention 'naturally' to the elements we wish him to take in, our imperatives to concentrate, memorize or learn are almost bound to fail. (Wood 1988, p.61)

Mindfulness Play encourages self-motivation in children by ensuring that activities are:

- intrinsically rewarding (they are not just fun for each child but also lead to a tangible change in self-belief – e.g. through the experience of mastering a skill)

- extrinsically rewarding (e.g. children notice a positive difference in how other people respond to their achievements in focusing, concentrating and calming)

- appropriate for the age and stage of the child (i.e. she should be developmentally ready)

- constructed so as to build upon the child's current knowledge and memory abilities, thereby minimising possible stresses about remembering the rules and procedures and ensuring that motivation is not inhibited by fear of negative evaluation or ridicule by others.

One of the main ways in which we can facilitate these aspects of motivation mindfully is by offering appropriate praise.

Praise and demonstration of pleasure in a child's abilities, perseverance, sense of fun and so on can be an excellent motivator for continued change and development, but it will be of little value if it is not genuine or has no personal meaning for the child. If praise does not resonate with her self-concept and self-evaluations she is very likely to reject it. Also, unrealistic or unjustified praise could set her up for experiencing low self-esteem if she tries to do things before she is ready or if it leads to her developing unrealistically high expectations of what she can achieve.

Similarly, it can be all too easy to offer praise that indicates the lesser achievements of others. An award for the fastest worker or best listener, for example, suggests that there are others in the group who are not so good at this and also gives little scope for further development ('If I am already the best, I don't need to think about that any more'). So, here are some alternatives which I believe are pivotal to the concept of Mindfulness Play. Each of these draws on our own ability for mindfulness and also encourages mindfulness in children.

- Acknowledge each child. A clear demonstration that we value each child as a unique individual can have far-reaching effects and yet can be conveyed to children in the simplest of ways – for example, by making sure that the children in the group have been acknowledged by name as they arrive, and by giving some indication of pleasure that they are there (a smile, a 'thumbs up' gesture). Telling a child that we enjoy her company or love talking with her emphasises the fact that she has a positive effect on us simply by being who she is and not because of what she does or doesn't say or do.

- Use genuine specific, descriptive praise whenever possible: 'I liked the way you really listened to what Josh had to say about following the rules of the game', 'I noticed that you were quietly encouraging Sam to come back to the group when he got distracted and that really worked because he calmed down straight away', 'Your "busy" picture really shows me what it must be like for you when it's hard to concentrate on one thing. This is what I call thoughtful' or 'You were ace at noticing your fidgety feelings and keeping them controlled during that game.'

- Acknowledge difficulties and empathise with the feelings: 'It looked as if it was hard for you to wait your turn. You had lots of great ideas to share! That must have been really frustrating for you!'

- Encourage children to give descriptive praise to each other ('What did you like about the way that Josh told us that?').

- Encourage descriptive *self*-praise ('I noticed some new things in that game and that means I was concentrating well' or 'I joined in with a new game and it was hard but I felt good afterwards').

- Express your admiration. This enables a child to self-evaluate in a wonderfully productive way: 'That's fantastic! How did you know how to do that?', 'I had no idea that you were so good at calming yourself/ knew so many games/were so artistic/could run so fast. Was that hard to learn?' or 'Tim said that you always remember people's birthdays – that's really impressive! How do you manage to do that?'

- Give non-verbal signals of approval and encouragement. A 'thumbs up', a wink or a smile across a room can be helpful for children who are self-conscious. You can show that you have noticed them without drawing the attention of other children in the group. This sort of 'private' praise is particularly helpful for children who are anxious and may be enough to break the train of thought that could lead to withdrawal or displays of frustration.

- Use acronyms and abbreviations. Christine Durham, in her book *Chasing Ideas* (2006), describes a useful way to make praise a fun interaction for older children. She suggests the use of acronyms and abbreviations such as VIP (very important proposition) or IT (insightful thinking). This could start as a game in itself – perhaps taking familiar acronyms and familiar sayings and encouraging children to make up 'secret' messages about their skills in focusing and concentrating. For example, VIP could be 'very imaginative problem-solver' or ACE could be 'a cool example'. Giving a child a 'thumbs up' sign and saying 'ACE' then becomes even more meaningful and fun.

- Encourage children to reflect on what happens outside the games sessions, picking up on the encounters and strategies that are working well and, in particular, any moments of difficulty that have been successfully negotiated.

- Use memory aids if necessary to help you to remember ideas that children have come up with during some of the games. Comment on these at a later time to show that you have really thought about what was said. Non-judgemental comments on past experiences and actions can be extremely motivating and self-affirming for children.

- Acknowledge and celebrate current strengths. Although some children might find it difficult to recognise their current abilities, achievements and talents, this is always a good starting point before moving on to thinking about targets for learning and future goals for self-development. Children generally have very little time in their lives to celebrate where they are at before moving on to the next challenge, the next learning target, the next physical achievement – almost as though we are telling them, 'Yes, well done, but that's still not quite good enough.'

There is one more aspect of praise that is significant in terms of group processes (this includes families). The *absence* of praise may have almost as much of a detrimental effect on some vulnerable children as the giving of negative comments. When a vulnerable child hears others in the group being praised by an important adult for attributes and talents which she admires but does not feel she possesses (and is not being praised for), this gives indirect information to that child about how the adult views her. So whilst we need to keep praise realistic and honest, we also need to find out what really matters to individual children. What do they most admire in others? What would they most like to be praised for? How could we support them in nurturing their wishes in this respect?

The ability to set goals and to 'aspire' to greater achievements is also, of course, another prime motivator. Children may need support in setting realistic goals with small, manageable steps, but even unrealistic goals can be acknowledged as a heartfelt wish or an exciting thought. Again, in Mindfulness Play we can encourage children to learn how to formulate steps towards a goal and to imagine situations 'as if' they had really happened.

Valuing children's views about a games session is also likely to foster increased motivation to engage more fully in the learning process, and a child's comments about a particular game/activity could guide you in choosing another one to address that specific issue or skill. Helping children to be reflective thinkers is a vital part of Mindfulness Play. Some children are naturally more reflective: they tend to take longer to respond to questions and problems and they will generally make fewer errors than an impulsive child. Games that allow children the opportunity to 'pause and reflect' in a constructive way can greatly aid the emergence of appropriate strategies and, as noted earlier, can result in remarkable insights that may otherwise be missed.

The next chapter explores the concept of foundation elements for well-being and how these are necessary for the building of skills in focusing, concentrating and calming.

5

Mindfulness Play and Well-Being

Key concepts

- Mindfulness Play is based on a model of well-being.

- Well-being relies on foundation elements, core abilities and specific skills.

- Foundation elements, abilities and skills are interconnected.

- Mindfulness Play involves awareness of the interconnections.

Mindfulness Play is based on a model of well-being

In the West, we have a tendency to separate out the components of well-being into physical, social, emotional and spiritual. Whilst these are all recognised as vital to a child's healthy development, the interconnectedness of these different aspects is not always acknowledged. A sense of well-being is also subjective and therefore difficult to measure. Perhaps partly in response to this, researchers have often focused on educational outcomes of well-being programmes carried out in schools. There is ample evidence from a variety of studies (e.g. Diamond and Lee 2011) that such programmes do have positive effects on academic achievement – something which we might intuitively have guessed. It would make sense, for example, that if a child is developing a healthy sense of 'self', feels well supported, is resilient enough to cope with minor setbacks, has a strong friendship group and is generally happy in school, then he is more likely to be able to focus his attention, to concentrate for increasing lengths of time and to enjoy and be able to capitalise on the learning environment.

However, the fact that well-being is difficult to measure should not deter us from making this a primary focus of our daily interactions with children, whether we be parents, carers, teachers or therapists or indeed are concerned with children's welfare in any other capacity.

Mindfulness Play is based on a model of integrated well-being that acknowledges the interplay between the physical, social, emotional and spiritual aspects of our lives. This model centres on eight *foundation elements* (Plummer 2007a, 2011). These generic foundation elements act as the bedrock for sets of *core abilities*, such as the ability to imagine, and *specific skills*, such as the skill of monitoring personal thoughts (see Chapter 6). Core abilities and specific skills can be targeted towards particular areas of intended learning or change – in this instance, focusing, concentrating and self-calming.

Foundation elements, abilities and skills are interconnected

A key component of this model is awareness of the connection between levels. This means that whichever area we are working on – specific skills, core abilities or foundation elements – we will also see repercussions on the other two levels. So, for example, if we help children to identify current strengths and to develop others in the foundation elements, this will support them in learning and sustaining specific skills; if we encourage identification and further development of core abilities, we will be helping children to 'feed' the foundation elements; if we highlight specific skills with creativity and integrity, then we can directly affect a child's perceptions of his core abilities and his strengths within the foundation elements.

Similarly, there are interconnections *within* levels. When working in the domain of one of the foundation elements, we will invariably see effects in other elements too. Core abilities will develop alongside each other, and working on developing and improving specific skills will lead to the enhancement of others. We will see the most profound effect if we specifically structure our support with conscious awareness of these interconnections.

Box 5.1 An image of the well-being model

Imagine that you and I have been invited to join a new community of well-being. We are offered adjoining plots of exactly the same size and told that we can build a single story building within this plot, containing eight rooms. We can make the rooms different sizes but the end result will be the same sized floor plan. Each of these rooms constitutes one of the well-being foundation elements. We are told that we can have walls between the rooms or we can have a more 'open plan' design if we like, with rooms flowing into each other. In order to complete our new homes to our desired specifications we will be given help from the current inhabitants of Well-being Town but we also need to develop and use our own 'core abilities' such as the ability to imagine, effective observation and listening skills, a degree of self-control and the ability to adapt to different environments. These abilities will help us to build our homes with mindfulness. The furnishings and fixtures of each of our homes are likely to be different although we might naturally share some items in common. The fixtures and furnishings represent the specific skills that, in effect, demonstrate our core abilities.

And finally, we can have any number of windows and doors to facilitate views and access to and from different rooms and to and from the outside world. These represent our levels of self-efficacy and mutuality. The final dwelling place will therefore also reflect our levels of self-awareness and our sense of living life mindfully.

We both construct our dwellings, and move in as soon as possible, in fact long before completion. Soon, I notice that you appear to be having a lot more fun than me in your new home! You help me to realise that two of my rooms need changing. 'Beyond self' is small and sparsely furnished and the adjacent 'self-reliance' room looks more like a fortress than the relaxing, comfortable space that I would like it to be. You help me to recognise that different rooms serve important functions at different stages in our lives. I knock down a wall, shift a bit of furniture, add some comfortable floor cushions and lo and behold I have a meditation room, large enough for friends to use as well.

Whatever our well-being homes look like at this moment in time they will inevitably continue to change, sometimes in subtle ways, sometimes more dramatically as we cope with life's ups and downs. Mindfulness Play is one way in which we can help children to construct their own well-being homes.

The eight foundation elements are: self-knowledge, self and others, self-acceptance, self-reliance, self-expression, self-confidence, self-awareness and 'beyond self'. The key features of these elements are based on cognitive processes, and involve: *developing, knowing, recognising, believing, feeling* and *understanding* (Plummer 2011).

1. SELF-KNOWLEDGE

This is about finding out who 'I' am and where I fit into the social world around me. Self-knowledge involves:

- understanding differences and commonalities – for example, how I am different from others in looks and character, or how I can have an interest in common with others

- knowing that I have many aspects to my personality

- developing and maintaining my personal values

- developing a sense of my personal history – my own 'life story'.

A strong sense of 'self' and a sense of belonging are vital elements of well-being. It is important for children to know something about their history and how they fit into family, friendship and community groups. Children love to hear and to tell stories about themselves. Familiar themes might be 'Tell me the story about when I was born' or 'What happened when I had to go to hospital when I was a baby?' or 'Do you remember when I got that prize/got bullied/fell over/climbed the tree...?' Even when adults have related the same story on several different occasions, there is often still a need to hear it many more times. This is a major way in which we learn about ourselves – by repeatedly hearing and telling our stories.

Mindfulness Play provides opportunities for children to tell their stories in an environment of respect.

Development of this foundation element contributes to the building of a child's 'awakened' relationship with himself.

2. SELF AND OTHERS

This involves:

- understanding the joys and challenges of relationships: learning to trust and to negotiate and cooperate with others; being able to see things from another person's perspective (empathy) and developing an understanding of how they might see me; learning respect and tolerance for other people's needs and views

- developing and maintaining my own identity as a separate person while still recognising the natural mutuality and interdependence inherent in relationships

- developing a sense of my family/cultural 'story'.

Clearly, it is important to help all children to negotiate social situations, connect with others and form appropriate friendships in ways that are suitable for their current developmental level and learning abilities. At the same time, we should also take into account the need to foster healthy self-esteem, self-reliance and self-respect. This balance between healthy connectedness with others and personal autonomy is described by developmental psychologist Susan Harter as 'mutuality' (Harter 1999, p.295). Mindfulness Play encourages mutuality in a natural and fun way.

Development of this foundation element enables children to work with or alongside other children and adults with awareness and sensitivity, to engage in shared attention activities and to direct their focus and concentration without being inappropriately distracted by others.

3. SELF-ACCEPTANCE

This involves:

- knowing my own strengths, recognising what can't be changed and recognising areas that I find difficult and may want to work on

- accepting that it is natural to make mistakes and that this is sometimes how we learn best

- feeling OK about my physical body.

Recognising our achievements and being able to accept sincere praise and compliments is an important aspect of self-acceptance. This element also involves recognising the areas that we can change or are already working on and those things that would be much more difficult to change or may even be impossible to change. Part of self-acceptance involves understanding the difference between making mistakes and failing. Young children are often not aware that older children and adults make mistakes too and that this can be a very productive way of learning – some of the most inspired inventors and scientists achieve their best creations through making mistakes in design and learning from them!

Our self-concept includes all aspects of how we see ourselves, and self-acceptance therefore also includes body awareness and feeling OK about our physical appearance.

Development of this foundation element helps children to recognise times when they are able to focus and concentrate successfully, to acknowledge times when this might be difficult because of distracting internal thoughts and feelings (especially when these are self-limiting thoughts such as 'I can't do this') or external circumstances (such as a noisy environment over which they have no control), and to develop the capacity to recognise and accept feedback from others in terms of their progress. It is also an important foundation element for enhancing positive body awareness so that children can, for example, let go of unwanted tension or focus on calm breathing and can learn to use body awareness in order to further develop their capacity for mindfulness.

4. SELF-RELIANCE

This involves:

- knowing how to take care of myself, both physically and emotionally

- building a measure of independence and self-motivation; believing that I have mastery over my life and can meet challenges as and when they arise

- reducing my reliance on other people's opinions and evaluations.

Of course, the skills needed to build self-reliance are acquired very gradually in childhood, but each step can be a tremendous boost to self-esteem and general well-being, especially if they are noted and celebrated. A child's physical achievements, such as being able to dress himself or ride a bike, are often acknowledged and celebrated, but there are other areas of self-reliance which may be missed by the child and by adults as well. These small triumphs of emotional self-care can be a powerful force for increased motivation, independent thinking, self-efficacy (Bandura 1977, 1989[1]) and emotional resilience, and we need to be on the lookout for them and encourage them just as much as the physical signs of self-reliance.

Mindfulness Play provides numerous opportunities for supporting children in their building of self-reliance. When children start to develop a degree of self-reliance, they are more able to enjoy the exciting and fun things in life and more ready to cope with things that are challenging or difficult.

Development of this foundation element promotes feelings of being in control and helps children in their growing abilities to anticipate and predict what might happen next, both as a consequence of their own behaviour and also as a consequence of other people's behaviour. Strengthening self-reliance also promotes motivation to focus, attend and self-calm.

---

1   Albert Bandura defined self-efficacy as the *belief* that we are capable of doing something and that we can influence events that affect our lives (Bandura 1977, 1989).

5. SELF-EXPRESSION

This involves:

- understanding that my interactions reflect my beliefs about myself and about others

- building and maintaining a sense of enjoyment and effectiveness in the act of communication

- developing creativity in self-expression and recognising and celebrating the unique and diverse ways in which we each express who we are.

Mindfulness Play provides children with the forum to express who they are in a playful and fun way and to formulate their thoughts and opinions in a safe environment. Development of this foundation element will help children to benefit from the focus and concentration required to communicate with others effectively and mindfully.

6. SELF-CONFIDENCE

This involves:

- developing a strong sense of self-efficacy (see foundation element 4 above)

- knowing that my opinions, thoughts and actions have value and that I have the right to express them

- developing my knowledge and skills so that I feel able to experiment with different methods of problem solving and can be flexible enough to alter my strategies if needed

- feeling strong enough to accept challenges and make choices

- feeling secure enough in myself to be able to cope with the unexpected.

We all have creative potential, but many of us fail to use it constructively. The amount of creativity we use is closely related to our self-concept. As children learn to tolerate the frustration of making mistakes and begin to experience success, they also start to trust in their own judgements and decisions more and more. This helps to confirm their abilities and self-worth and gives them confidence to know that they will be able to cope with future difficulties effectively.

Once again, Mindfulness Play offers children the chance to experiment, take on progressively bigger challenges, be creative in constructing and trying out new games, take on different roles within games and cope with unexpected outcomes.

Development of this foundation element enables children to cope more effectively with distractions, to make informed choices about how and when to focus their attention and to build effective strategies for self-calming.

7. SELF-AWARENESS

This involves:

- developing the ability to be focused in the here and now rather than absorbed in negative thoughts about the past or future (see core abilities, Chapter 6).

- recognising my feelings as they arise

- understanding that emotional, mental and physical changes are a natural part of my life

- being aware of the normal fluctuations in how I feel and how these link to my thoughts and behaviour

- recognising that I have choices about how I think, feel and behave

- developing and maintaining emotional intelligence.[2]

Self-awareness is the cornerstone of realistic self-evaluation and is an inherent part of Mindfulness Play. In order to be constructively self-aware, children need to be able to concentrate and focus on what their senses are telling them, noting changes and recognising that they have some control over the way they feel and behave. Mindfulness Play contributes to this process by offering a forum in which feelings are acknowledged, valued and openly discussed in a non-judgemental way. By learning to value their own feelings and by facing difficult or confusing situations and coping with them successfully, children will be able to meet new challenges and develop their skills confidently and creatively, so further strengthening their feelings of well-being. They will also develop a healthy level of 'emotional resilience': the ability to cope with

---

2   Daniel Goleman suggests that emotional intelligence involves the ability to recognise and understand our own emotions and those of others, the ability to manage our emotions effectively and the ability to motivate ourselves (Goleman 1996, pp.43–4). Emotional intelligence within this model of well-being therefore also includes self-reliance (foundation element 4) and links with foundation element 2 (self and others).

temporary feelings of helplessness, frustration or upset without being engulfed by them or experiencing them as failure.

Development of this foundation element enables children to be able to switch attention effectively between internal and external stimuli, to monitor their internal 'self-talk'[3] and to calm themselves both physically and mentally.

8. BEYOND SELF

This involves:

- deepening my awareness and engagement with other people, with life and with my inner self. This might manifest in a number of ways such as a strong sense of connection with music, art, or the wonders of the universe, or a transpersonal/spiritual element to our lives which may or may not be based in religious beliefs

- developing an ability to focus and reflect upon realities beyond 'the self'

- acceptance of living with a degree of uncertainty and '*not* knowing' in life

- developing my ability to imagine.

Many children have a natural spiritual element to their lives and an ability to be totally 'in the moment' but may not feel comfortable in talking about this experience with others. In Mindfulness Play, such experiences may well become more overtly described and commented on. This puts facilitators in the unique position of being able to acknowledge and celebrate this remarkable capacity and help children to appreciate the wonder of sometimes simply 'being' – of staying present in the moment without striving to achieve a future goal and of joyfulness in a sense of connection with their inner life and with others. Development of this foundation element also promotes the development and understanding of empathy.

The next chapter explores the *core abilities* that are enhanced by development of the foundation elements and which also contribute to the strengthening of these elements.

---

3   An important aspect of self-talk is the 'genre' in which we tell our story (see foundation element 1). This is *how* we tell ourselves about who we are, how we feel and what we are able or not able to do. This aspect of our story will have a profound effect on how we behave, how we learn and how we relate to other people.

6

Control, Adaptability and Effectiveness

Key concepts

- There are five sets of core abilities necessary for focusing, concentrating and self-calming.

- Specific skills can be fostered in order to enhance the core abilities.

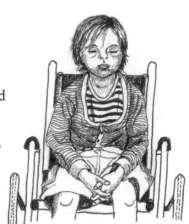

There are five sets of core abilities necessary for focusing, concentrating and self-calming

Within the well-being model presented in the previous chapter, there are several sets of core abilities. Five of these are particularly relevant to focusing, concentrating and calming. These are: self-control, adaptability, effective observation, effective listening and imagination. As with the foundation elements, these abilities are, in fact, fairly generic and are central to a number of different aspects of well-being (see Plummer 2011).

SELF-CONTROL

This includes the ability to have some control over our feelings and thoughts and the ways in which we expresses them, the ability to tolerate waiting and manage impulsivity, the ability to consciously switch attention from one stimulus to another by choice and the ability to persevere with difficult tasks.

The ability to maintain focus, through self-awareness and self-control, leads to concentration. Effective concentration contributes to perseverance, which in turn will increase the likelihood of successfully completing a task.

ADAPTABILITY

This involves the ability to adapt to new situations and changes in contexts, the ability to monitor and adjust actions, feelings and thoughts according to realistic assessments of personal progress and the ability to adapt to obstacles and challenges, such as a demanding listening environment. Adaptability not only enables us to move from one focus of attention to another appropriately but also allows us to attend to more than one stimulus at the same time. This divided attention often consists of a mixture of an internal stimulus (e.g. a memory) and an external stimulus. So, for example, we can link a current challenging event with the memory of a similar past experience that we handled well in order to feel confident about coping with it effectively again this time.

EFFECTIVE LISTENING

This includes the ability to really hear what others are saying and to reflect on what is heard. Effective listening inevitably includes self-control – for example the ability to focus on what is being said by others without allowing our own thoughts to dominate.

EFFECTIVE OBSERVATION

This includes the ability to observe and to reflect on details within our environment, non-verbal aspects of interactions and our own behaviour, and to expand our awareness of the context of the object of our attention.

IMAGINATION

The ability to imagine is an important aspect of learning, of creativity and problem solving and also of empathy – the ability to see things from another person's point of view and to be aware of others' needs. Imagination allows us to be more effective in directing our attention both internally and externally.

As already noted, the development of imagination is evident from a very early age in various aspects of play. Observation and listening skills, self-control and adaptability also build gradually.

Specific skills can be fostered in order to enhance the core abilities

Specific skills (competencies) manifest as the appropriate behaviours which demonstrate the core abilities. For example, in order to be able to *control* impulsivity, I may need to develop skills of:

- self-rewarding
- making appropriate choices
- monitoring physical sensations

- monitoring my internal 'chatter'

- pausing and focusing on a specific stimulus (e.g. focusing on my breathing).

In relation to the core ability of being able to *adapt* to a demanding listening environment that requires increased attention focus, any or all of the following specific skills may be utilised:

- problem-solving skills such as linking cause and effect, trying out different strategies, choosing and rejecting strategies appropriately

- appropriate use of requests such as asking for repetition of an instruction

- changing posture in order to observe/hear more effectively

- negotiating with peers to facilitate turn-taking and thereby reduce distractions

- utilising a personally effective strategy such as requesting to sit nearer to the speaker.

The core abilities involve not only actual competency or mastery of skills but also positive perception of self-efficacy. Bandura (see p.52) suggested that people who have perceptions of high self-efficacy often do better than those who have equal ability but less belief in themselves. They are more likely to persevere with difficult tasks, use more effective problem-solving strategies, set themselves more demanding goals and focus less on the possible consequences of failure.

Engaging in Mindfulness Play can be an excellent way of building competency (specific skills) and encouraging a sense of self-efficacy. As discussed in Chapter 4, however, it is important to talk with children about what competency truly means in terms of different skills being mastered at different ages and stages. It can be all too easy to foster unrealistic expectations so that children cannot tolerate natural mistakes.

It is also important to be aware of how the experience of playing games can itself contribute to increasing or decreasing feelings of self-efficacy, and we need to ensure that such activities are carefully structured to take this into account. Some of the fears that children may be facing in even the simplest of activities include worries about personal outcome (will I fail?), evaluation apprehension (will I embarrass myself?), feelings of low general efficacy (will this help?), and low self-efficacy (will I feel useless?). These considerations bring us back full circle to the whole concept of Mindfulness Play and to Charles Tart's idea of mindfulness as perceptual intelligence: the awakened ability to 'see more accurately and discriminatingly and so behave more appropriately toward others and toward our inner selves...' (Tart 1994, p.5; see Chapter 3).

In summary, Mindfulness Play is based on a model of well-being and perceptual intelligence.

It involves:

- adults and children sharing activities in a meeting place which bridges our diverse worlds

- developing an awakened relationship with ourselves and with others

- paying attention to the inner world of our own images and ideas

- focusing mindfully on the outer world of people, objects and events

- creating a nurturing environment for children's well-being

- understanding and respecting children's rituals and images in play

- celebrating each child's uniqueness, talents and insights.

Part Two

Focusing and Calming
Games and Activities

7

Choosing Groups, Pairs, Leaders and Order of Play

For the purpose of these games, we want to avoid placing children in a position where they are anxiously waiting to be picked or where the same groups or pairs consistently choose to work together. Here are just a few ideas.

To choose a leader

- Have names in a hat or in separate balloons. Children pick a name or pop a balloon to see who is the leader for that session. This ensures that everyone eventually gets a turn.

- Take turns according to dates of birth (e.g. using just the date in the month).

- Play 'Lek shey, lek toh' (long finger, short finger). This version is based on a game from Burma (Dunn 1978, p.20) and is suitable for

3–6 players of any age. Player A encloses the fingers of his right hand with his left hand so that only the tips of the right fingers are showing and it is difficult to tell the difference between them. Players pick a finger each. The one who chooses the middle finger becomes the leader. When it is time to change leaders, it is this child who becomes player A.

- Play 'Up or Down' in groups of three. This version is based on a game from Pakistan (Dunn 1978, p.18). Players hold hands in a circle and swing their arms in rhythm for a short time. At a given signal, all players let go of each other's hands and quickly place their right hands on top of their left hands, either palms facing upwards or palms facing downwards. If two players have their fingers placed one way and the other has his fingers placed differently (e.g. two up and one down), the latter is the leader. If they are all the same, they play again.

Adaptations

- Gradually increase the number of arm swings before everyone lets go.

- Use a variety of auditory or visual signals for letting go of hands, such as bells, musical instruments, whisper, head movement, frown.

- The leader from this play session gives the signal next time and therefore doesn't take part in the circle for choosing the next leader.

To choose pairs

- Count round half the circle, then start again. The ones work together, twos work together, etc.

- Put two sets of matching objects in a 'lucky dip' box. Children draw out an object and find their partner who has a matching object.

- Children stand in a circle with eyes closed and arms outstretched. They walk across the circle until they meet someone else.

To choose groups

- Sit in a large circle. Count round in sets of two or four or however many small groups are needed. Ones then work together, twos work together, etc.

- Count round the circle using colour names, with as many different colours as are needed for the number of groups.

- Deal out playing cards – for example, all the clubs in one group and diamonds in the other.

To choose the order of play

This is based on 'Nawa kuji' (string lots), a game from Japan (Dunn 1978, p.26). The unadapted game is suitable for 2–6 players aged seven upwards.

- Leaving a long piece of string at the start, the game coordinator folds a length of string to make the same number of loops as there are players. He then holds the string tightly in one hand, leaving the loops showing from the top of his fist and the long piece showing from the bottom of his fist. Players should not be able to tell which is the first loop and which is the last loop. Each player then hooks their middle finger into a loop. The coordinator slowly pulls the long piece of string. The first loop will get smaller and the person with his finger in this loop will be the first person to play. The second player is identified in the same way and so on until there are no more loops.

Adaptation

- Use coloured silk squares knotted together to make scarves of different lengths. Cram them into a container so that only one end of each scarf is showing. Players each take an end and everyone pulls out the scarves at the same time. Count the squares to see the order of play.

8

Warm-Ups and Ice-Breakers

Warm-ups and ice-breakers foster group cohesion and help to develop a group identity. They encourage children to interact with each other and help them to feel that they have been acknowledged by everyone else in the group. They act as a ritual to mark the beginning of a session and to ensure that each person has fully 'arrived' in the group.

As with all the games and activities in this book, those within this section can also be extended and adapted to be used specifically for enhancing the abilities and skills needed for focusing, concentrating and self-calming. Many of the suggestions for exapnsion ideas can also be used interchangeably.

What's my name?

⑦

🕐 10 minutes

♦ ♦ ♦

◯◯◯

☑ self and others (E)

☑ effective listening (A)

☑ asking questions (S)

The basic game

Players write their name (or how they would like to be known) on a sticky label. They hide the label somewhere on their own clothes – for example, in the top of their sock, in a pocket, under their collar or on the sole of their shoe.

Children try to find as many names as possible (within a time limit suitable for the size of the group) without touching anyone. They can only ask questions such as 'Is it on the sole of your shoe?' or 'Can you show me underneath your right foot?' They either write down all the names that they find or try to remember them.

When the time limit is up, everyone stands or sits in a circle. The game coordinator stands behind each person in turn and everyone tries to remember that person's name.

Adaptations

Throw a soft cushion around the group. Each child says her own name when she catches it. After everyone has had a turn, go round again. This time the rest of the group say the name of the child who catches the cushion.

Use a weighted or strangely shaped soft object so that everyone is likely to have some difficulty catching it – a fun way to even out the ability levels in the group.

Use an imaginary object such as a large, heavy ball or a delicate paper bird.

Put name labels in a bowl. Each child picks out another child's name and tries to find that person in the group and present them with the label.

Make two sets of animal picture labels: one for children to wear and one to put in the bowl. Children pick an animal label from the bowl and find the matching picture worn by a group member.

Expansion ideas

What helps you to remember other people's names?

Why is it important to try to remember people's names?

What do you feel like when other people remember your name?

What skills are needed for this game? How might these skills be helpful in other activities?

Research meanings of names and encourage children to design personal emblems or badges.

Notes

Remember me

⑦   ☑ self-awareness (E)

🕐 10 minutes   ☑ self-control (A)

🚶 🚶   ☑ taking turns (S)

💬

The basic game Players sit in a circle. The first player says her own name. The second player says the first player's name and her own name, the third player says the first two names, and her own name, and so on around the group.

Adaptations Players can prompt each other if needed.

Names are said in time to rhythmic clapping to keep the momentum going.

Alternate children in the circle take turns to say their own name and the name of the person sitting on their right. This second child claps twice but does not speak. If anyone claps when they should be speaking or speaks when they should be clapping, the whole process changes direction.

Expansion ideas Is it harder or easier to remember names when you are concentrating on something else as well?

Does this apply to other tasks? Does it depend on what the task is?

In later games sessions this could be linked with trying to remember calming strategies. For example, if I'm trying to fix something and it's hard to do, it will be even harder if I get frustrated, but easier if I remember to stay focused and calm.

Notes

Party guests

⑨

🕐 10 minutes

🧍 🧍 🧍

💬💬

☑	self-awareness (E)
☑	effective listening (A)
☑	memory strategies (S)

The basic game

Each member of the group thinks of a true fact that she would like other group members to know about her. This should be a personal statement about an ability, like or dislike. Players introduce themselves to each other in pairs and share their personal statements. All pairs then walk around the room together, introducing their partners and responding to introductions from others. For example, 'This is Moira and she loves swimming', 'Hello, Moira, I'm Jan and this is Ryan. He's really good at drawing cartoons.'

Adaptation

Players invent something amazing to say about their partner, based on what is already known about her interests and personality. For example, 'This is Moira and she is the youngest person ever to win an Olympic gold medal.'

Expansion ideas

Children don't normally introduce each other in such a formal way, but when might such formal introductions be used?

How else might we get to know facts about each other?

How does it feel to hear someone else introduce you in this way?

What helps you to remember important things about other people?

Talk about appreciating and respecting our own and other people's talents and abilities.

Notes

Guess the voice

⑦   ☑ self-expression (E)
🕐 10 minutes   ☑ adaptability (A)
👤 👤 👤   ☑ perception (S)
💬

The basic game

Players stand or sit in a circle. Each player invents a unique vocal call – for example, a combination of vowels with different intonation patterns or a hum or a whistle. The whole group listens to each call in turn as the players say their first name and then their chosen sound.

One person stands in the centre of the circle with a blindfold on. The game coordinator silently chooses someone to make her call. The person in the centre tries to name the caller. If she gets it right, she can have a second turn.

Each person has a maximum of two turns before the coordinator chooses another person to sit in the centre.

Adaptations

Callers recite one line of a well-known song or a pre-chosen phrase that all the children are able to say/remember.

Two people stand in the centre and can confer about the name of the caller.

The person who was last in the centre can choose the next caller.

Everyone changes seats before the caller is chosen.

The players are split into pairs to practise their calls. One child from each pair then stands in the centre of the circle and is blindfolded. On a signal, their partners make their chosen calls. The players who are blindfolded have to move carefully around the circle until they find their partner.

Expansion ideas

What helps us to listen? Is it easier or harder for you to listen when you are blindfolded? Why is this?

How do we recognise individual voices? What makes our voices different?

What might happen if we all sounded exactly the same?

What words can we use to describe different voices (e.g. deep, gruff, loud, soft, like chocolate)? Keep these descriptions very general, rather than specific to individual children.

Does your voice change according to how you are feeling? How does it change?

Notes

Signs and signatures

⑦

☑ self-awareness (E)

🕐 5 minutes

☑ effective observation (A)

👤 👤 👤

☑ understanding other perspectives (S)

💬💬

The basic game

Players sit in a circle. The first player says her name accompanied by a movement/gesture (e.g. head movement, clapping, making sweeping gesture with both hands). The next child introduces the previous child (using her name and gesture) and then says her own name accompanied by her own gesture.

This is _____ **and I am** _____ .

Finish with everyone saying and gesturing their own name at the same time.

Adaptations

Players say their own name and think of a gesture but do not need to introduce anyone.

Play the game standing up and include large movements such as jump back, shake leg, hop.

Teach the children specific signs, such as finger spelling for their initials or signs for different animals.

In smaller groups, players can try to remember the names and gestures of as many previous players as possible (in a similar way to the game 'Remember me' on p.70).

Expansion ideas

Does the gesture reflect your personality in some way? Talk about the differences and similarities between how you see yourself and how you think others see you.

If you had a different name, would you choose a different gesture? Do you think other people would also link this gesture with your name?

Think of a family member or a friend. What gesture might she choose to go with her name? Would you choose a different gesture for her or the same one?

Notes

Parachute name game

⑤   ☑ self and others (E)

🕐 10 minutes   ☑ self-control (A)

👤 👤 👤   ☑ cooperation (S)

💬

Parachute games can be played with just two people or up to 40 with a full-sized chute, and you can be endlessly creative: a parachute can be the sea, the sky, a mountain, a lake, a caterpillar, a tent – anything that you want it to be! As with any games involving the use of equipment, these games should be supervised by adults at all times. Small children can easily get themselves tangled up in a large chute. At the very least, this can be a scary experience. In order to maintain a good grip on the parachute, roll the edge up and tuck your fingers underneath the rolled fabric.

The basic game

Players hold the parachute at waist level. A large soft ball is placed in the middle of the parachute. The game coordinator says the name of each player in turn and everyone tries to send the ball across the circle to that person.

Adaptations

Players crouch down around the outside of the parachute, holding tightly to the edge. The game coordinator says, 'One, two, three, up parachute,' and everyone jumps up, making the parachute mushroom into the air. The coordinator quickly calls the names of two players who must swap places by running underneath the parachute before it floats back down. (Remind the children to be careful not to bump into each other!)

Invite all the children to lie still under the parachute while facilitators gently waft it up and down over the top of them and the children say their name in turn.

Sit around the outside edge of the parachute and introduce each other or pass a smile or a hand squeeze around the circle.

Expansion ideas

Was it easy or difficult to make the ball move in the right direction? Why was this?

Our names are a very important part of who we are. How do we hear our names used? Lovingly, angrily, accusingly, melodiously? How would we like to hear them used in this group? Can you always tell what someone is feeling when they say your name? How can you tell? Are you always right?

When is it OK to shout out someone's name? When is it not OK?

Notes

Additional notes and reflections

9

Focusing Attention

Duck duck goose

⑤   ☑ self and others (E)

🕐 5 minutes   ☑ self-control (A)

🕴 🕴 🕴   ☑ tolerating frustration (S)

💬

The basic game   Players sit or stand in a circle facing each other. One player is the fox. He walks slowly around the outside of the circle, tapping each player on the shoulder and saying 'duck'. When the fox taps a player and says 'goose', the fox and the goose run around the circle in opposite directions to see who can get back to the empty place first. The player left out of the circle then walks slowly around the outside and chooses another goose. Play continues until everyone has had the chance to be a goose and a fox or until the players are ready to stop!

Adaptations   The fox walks around the circle using different adjectives to describe the ducks – for example, 'big duck', 'little duck', 'happy duck', 'sad duck' – and the other players listen out for a pre-chosen adjective to start running – for example, 'quick duck'.

One player walks around the circle saying words from a particular category (e.g. animals). When he names something from another category (e.g. fruit), the race begins.

Players listen out for the names of characters in a well-known story.

Players hop in opposite directions to get to the available space.

Mark the empty space with a picture so that the fox and the goose know where they are headed.

Expansion ideas   How easy or difficult was it for you to know when to run? Why was this?

How easy or difficult was it for you to wait to be picked? Do you normally wait until someone says something to you before joining in with a conversation or with a discussion in class? How is this similar/different to waiting your turn in a game?

How easy or difficult was it for players to avoid bumping into each other? Why do you think this?

Notes

Pass a smile

⑤

☑ self and others (E)

🕐 5 minutes

☑ self-control (A)

♦ ♦ ♦

☑ tolerating waiting (S)

💬

This is a fun group game but it can also be played with just two people.

The basic game

Players sit in a circle. Everyone tries to look very solemn. A child is chosen to start off a smile. He sends a smile to the person sitting next to him. This person smiles then 'zips' their lips in order to 'hold' the smile. He then turns to the next person and unzips the smile to pass it on! When the smile has been around the circle once, the group have a go at passing another smile but this time even more quickly.

Adaptations

'Throw' a smile across the circle. Everyone has to stay on the alert to catch it.

Pass a frown or a look of surprise.

Alternate between two different expressions.

Expansion ideas

How easy or difficult is it for you to control the expression on your face? Why is this?

Do you always know what expression you are showing? For example, do you know when you are frowning?

How does your body feel when you smile? What makes you smile? Can you tell the difference between a genuine smile and a pretend one or an 'unkind' smile? How can you tell the difference?

How does your body feel when you frown? What sorts of things cause you to frown?

What helps you to be a good 'observer'?

Think of some situations when having good observation skills would be very useful.

Notes

Shepherds and sheep

⑦
🕐 10 minutes
👤 👤
💬

☑ self-acceptance (E)
☑ imagination (A)
☑ flexible thinking (S)

The basic game | Children work together in pairs. One is the shepherd and the other is the sheep. The sheep wears a blindfold or covers his eyes. The shepherd steers the sheep into its pen (a square marked out with masking tape) by using changes in pitch or volume only. For example, humming with a rising pitch for 'go left', a falling pitch for 'go right' and a level pitch for 'straight ahead'. Once the sheep is safely in the pen, the pairs swap over but start from a different position in the room, playground, etc.

Adaptations | Use more subtle, appropriate pitch changes for 'yes', 'nearly right', 'wrong way', etc.

Steer the sheep to its pen using changes in volume or clapping.

Sheep keep their eyes uncovered and are directed by non-verbal signals such as waving for 'go left' and standing on one leg for 'go right'.

Expansion ideas | Was it easier to be the sheep or the shepherd? Why was this?

What helps you to listen effectively/observe effectively?

What skills did the shepherds and the sheep need for this game?

Notes

Switch over

⑤   ☑ self-awareness (E)

🕑 5 minutes   ☑ self-control (A)

👤 👤 👤   ☑ coping with distractions (S)

💬

It is important to be aware of any cultural differences in the appropriateness of different levels of eye contact when playing this game.

The basic game   Pairs sit facing each other. They choose who is A and who is B. They must keep eye contact and try to keep a straight face. The game coordinator waits until everyone is quiet and then says, 'switch over', at which point person A tries to make person B laugh in any way he can without touching the other player. At any time the coordinator can say, 'switch over' again and the players have to swap roles.

Adaptations   Players lie down on the floor in a circle with heads nearly touching in the centre and feet facing towards the outside of the circle, their hands resting gently on their stomachs. The first person starts off by saying 'ha!', the second says 'ha ha!', the third says 'ha ha ha!', and so on, going as fast as possible until someone starts to laugh for real. Then everyone has to wait for silence before another player starts off a round of 'ho!'

This can also be played with each person lying with their head on someone else's stomach. The movement involved in saying 'ha!' can cause laughter before the round gets very far at all!

Expansion ideas   How easy or difficult was it for you to keep eye contact? Why was this?

Was it easy or difficult to stop yourself from laughing? Why was this?

How do you feel when you have had a 'fit of the giggles'? Talk about the difference between laughing *at* someone and laughing *with* someone.

Is it possible to make yourself laugh or smile just by thinking about something funny?

Notes

Circle move

⑤   ☑ self-awareness (E)

🕐 5 minutes   ☑ effective observation (A)

♦ ♦ ♦   ☑ pausing and refocusing (S)

💬

The basic game	Players sit in a circle. One person starts off a movement such as a shoulder shake. Each player copies this in turn until everyone is making the same movement. Then everyone stops in turn until the circle is still. The person sitting to the left of the first player then starts a different movement and sends this around the group in the same way. Do this as many times as feels comfortable, varying the speed.
Adaptations	Two players sitting on opposite sides of the circle start off two different movements at the same time and send them in the same direction or in opposite directions.
	Players 'throw' the movement to each other across the circle by gaining eye contact with another player.
	Lengthen the period of stillness between the end of one movement and the start of the next.
Expansion ideas	How easy or difficult was it for you to keep focused on the movement? Why was this?
	What were you doing/thinking/feeling while you were waiting for your turn?
Notes	

3D noughts and crosses

⑤   ☑ self-confidence (E)

🕑 10 minutes   ☑ adaptability (A)

👤 👤   ☑ sustaining alertness (S)

💬

The basic game
Draw out a large chalk grid of nine squares (3 × 3) on the playground or mark it out on the floor using masking tape. Mark three beanbags with a cross and three with a circle. Take turns to toss the bags on to the grid, trying to get three crosses or three circles in a row.

Adaptations
Place coloured squares or pictures of everyday objects, animal pictures, sound pictures in the grid. When a child manages to get a beanbag into a square, he names the colour/object/makes the sound.

If you are working with a group of six or more children, then each child can hold his beanbag with the nought/cross clearly visible and jump into the squares instead of throwing the bag. (This can be played as a team game or simply for fun with no attempt at having a winning team.)

Throw three beanbags randomly on to the grid and wherever they land fully in a square, say the sounds/name the objects or make up a story.

Expansion ideas
How easy or difficult is it to get three noughts or three crosses in a row? Why is this?

Is it easier to work as a team or on your own? Why?

How difficult or easy is it to stand still when you are waiting for your turn? Why do you think this is?

Notes

Important names

⑦

🕐 5 minutes

† † †

💬

☑ self-acceptance (E)

☑ imagination (A)

☑ sustaining joint attention (S)

This game could also be used as an ice-breaker or warm-up activity.

I use a Tibetan bell for the adapted version. Children ring it just once and say their name as the chime resonates around the room. It can add a wonderful sense of grandeur and dignity to the sound of each name.

The basic game   Each person chooses a special word to describe himself, beginning with the first letter of his name (e.g. energetic Edward, happy Henry). Stand in a circle and use a softball or beanbag to throw. On the first round, the catcher says his own special name. On the second round, the thrower calls out another player's special name as he throws the ball/beanbag to him.

Adaptations   Players choose special names to reflect particular talents (not necessarily using the first letter of their name).

Players choose names for each other.

Use a small bell with a clapper. The first player carries the bell slowly across the circle to another player, trying not to let it ring. The person who receives the bell rings it loudly and says his special name (younger children can just say their first name). He then carries the bell across the circle to another player and so on until everyone has had a turn.

Expansion ideas   Think about the enjoyment of saying and hearing your own name.

How can you celebrate your name?

Take time to reflect on the qualities in yourself that you really like.

Why is self-respect important?

How do we show self-respect and respect for others?

Notes

Sleeping bear

⑤   ☑ self-awareness (E)

🕐 10 minutes   ☑ self-control (A)

👤 👤 👤   ☑ tolerating frustration (S)

💬

The basic game   The game coordinator chooses the first person to be the bear. This person sits on a chair in the middle of the circle or at the far end of the room, blindfolded. A bunch of keys is placed under the chair. The game coordinator chooses a player to creep up to the chair and steal the keys before the bear can point at him. If he manages to get the keys, then he becomes the new bear.

Adaptation   Two players at a time cross the room from opposite ends. They both keep their eyes shut. One is the hunter and one is the bear. They must both move slowly and cautiously and listen out for each other. The hunter tries to catch the bear and the bear tries to stay away from the hunter.

Expansion ideas   How easy or difficult is it for you to move slowly and quietly?

How easy or difficult is it to hear someone moving when you have your eyes closed?

Talk about self-control and self-awareness.

Talk about the difference between listening with full attention and hearing noises without fully attending.

Notes

All birds fly

⑥

🕐 5 minutes

† † †

💬

☑ self-confidence (E)

☑ adaptability (A)

☑ ignoring distractions (S)

The basic game | The aim is for the caller to 'catch players out' by getting them to flap their arms at the wrong time. A chosen player starts the game by flapping his arms like a bird and saying 'all birds fly'. All other players in the group flap their arms in response. The caller then names a mixture of birds, animals and objects in a random order, flapping his arms every time – for example, 'eagles fly', 'sparrows fly', 'monkeys fly', 'chairs fly', 'crows fly'. The rest of the group should only flap their arms when a bird is called. If any player flaps when an animal or an object is called, he has to stand still for the next two calls.

Each caller has ten turns before handing over to another caller (fewer if you are playing in a large group).

Adaptations | The same game could be played with 'all fish swim'. The caller makes a swimming gesture with one hand.

The time for standing still can be extended so that players experience waiting for longer periods.

Expansion ideas | Was this easy or difficult? What helped you to control your responses?

What were you thinking/feeling when you were waiting to join in again?

Is it easy or difficult to flap your arms for every word when you are the caller? Why do you think this is?

Notes

Mixing it up

⑤   ☑ self-awareness (E)

🕐 5 minutes   ☑ self-control (A)

👤 👤 👤   ☑ tolerating frustration (S)

💬

The basic game | This is another variation of 'Simon says'. The game coordinator demonstrates simple movements for players to follow, such as 'stand on one leg', 'touch your ear', 'wave', 'clap'. When the instruction is 'do this', then players copy the movement. When the instruction is 'do that', everyone should stand still. Anyone who moves by mistake must stand still for the next two calls.

Adaptations | Instead of standing still when mistakes are made, players continue to join in but move to an inner circle. It is likely that all players will be in this circle before very long!

Play 'Simon says' while holding on to a parachute. Movements will be based on leg, head or whole body movements – for example, stand on one leg, nod your head, shake your shoulders, shake your foot.

Vary the speed at which the calls are made.

Expansion ideas | Is it easy or difficult to listen, think and do something all at the same time? What could make it easier?

Talk about self-awareness and self-control.

When we repeat something often enough, we begin not to notice what we are doing. Why is this useful? When might it not be useful?

Sometimes our thoughts become automatic too. Automatic thoughts can sometimes be useful – they can save us thinking time! But if they are unhelpful thoughts, then we can learn to recognise these and begin to take control of them.

Notes

Sound tracking

⑤   ☑ self and others (E)

🕐 10 minutes   ☑ self-control (A)

🚶 🚶   ☑ controlling focus of attention (S)

💬

The basic game   The players sit silently in the centre of a darkened room with their eyes closed. The game coordinator hides a ticking clock in the room. Each player tries to locate the clock through listening only. The player who is the most accurate in his description of where the clock is (e.g. next to the door, on top of the bookcase) takes the next turn to hide the clock.

Adaptations   The clock is hidden before players enter the room.

Blindfolded players all point in the direction of the clock at the same time. The game coordinator decides who is the most accurate.

Two clocks are placed in different locations and players have to find both of them.

Use a hidden CD player to play music very quietly.

Players sit with their eyes closed and try to identify as many different sounds as possible (e.g. a ticking clock, the sound of breathing, traffic noises outside, the rain on the window).

This can be a visual game. Using two identical objects, show the players one and tell them that the other has been placed in plain view in the room somewhere. Players all stand or sit on one side of the room and see if they can spot the identical object without moving.

Expansion ideas   How easy or difficult is it to sit very still and listen? What makes it easier? What makes it harder?

Did you hear noises that you hadn't noticed before?

When is it useful to be able to choose what we listen to and ignore other sounds around us? What might make this difficult?

What sounds do you like to listen to? What sounds in the environment don't you like?

Put your hands over your ears. What can you hear?

Notes

'Eye' spy

⑦   ☑ self and others (E)

🕐 10 minutes   ☑ effective observation (A)

♦ ♦ ♦   ☑ selective attention (S)

💬💬💬

The basic game	Players walk around the room and meet each other. Each time they meet up with someone, they stay and look at each other's eyes for at least 30 seconds, taking turns to describe exactly what the other person's eyes look like – not just the main colour but as many other details as possible.
Adaptation	Children use mirrors to draw their own eyes and colour them in. The group tries to guess the owners of the drawings.
Expansion ideas	How easy or difficult was it to look into someone's eyes for 30 seconds?
	Did you notice anything new about how our eyes are structured?
	How can eye contact help when we communicate with each other?
	What do you like about your eyes?
	When you walk, do you look down at the ground or do you look around you?
	Look around the room. Can you see anything that you have never noticed before?
Notes	

Body focus

⑤   ☑ self-reliance (E)

🕐 10 minutes   ☑ self-control (A)

♦ ♦ ♦   ☑ monitoring physical sensations (S)

💬

Although this is, of course, an activity rather than a game, it is included here as a good starting point for encouraging self-awareness and focus. This is an exercise commonly taught as part of mindfulness meditation (see, for example, Tart 1994 or Kabat-Zinn 1996).

This activity can be done lying down or seated. Read each part slowly and calmly with plenty of pauses to allow children time to follow your instructions.

The basic activity   When you are ready, let your eyes close gently and settle yourself into a comfortable position.

Notice the feel of your body on the floor (in the chair)... Now start to notice your feet... Put all your attention on your feet and really notice what they feel like. Maybe they feel warm or cold; perhaps they are numb or itchy...tight or relaxed. Just notice whatever you can feel in your feet...

Now gently move your thoughts from your feet to the lower part of your legs. Let your thoughts leave your feet and just move very easily to your legs. Notice whatever feeling is there just at this moment... There are no right or wrong feelings... Whatever you can feel is OK... When your mind drifts off into other thoughts, just gently bring it back to noticing your body.

Now move up to your knees...and then the top part of your legs and notice whatever feelings are there... Now start to notice your body, feel what's happening when you breathe gently in and out... Start to think about your shoulders... Notice all the feelings around your neck and your head...

Let your thoughts go gently to your back...all along the length of your back... Thinking about your arms now. Just notice whatever is there...and down the length of your arms into your hands... Notice all your fingers one by one. Whatever is there, just notice it...

Now, keep noticing your body and start to listen to whatever sounds there are around you... Begin to move your hands and feet a little bit... When you feel ready, open your eyes and look around you... Lie or sit quietly for a short while before stretching and having a yawn.

Adaptations

Encourage children to try out different brief focusing exercises using their imagination for different image modalities. Even if these images prove difficult to hold on to at first, continued practice will aid the ability to focus successfully and to bring the mind back from its natural wanderings. Children can practise extending the time for which they can keep their focus on the images. The more simple the image, the more focused we need to be in order to keep it 'in mind'. Here are just a few examples:

- Visual

  - Imagine the front door of your home.

  - Imagine a pen slowly writing your name on a piece of paper.

  - Imagine different shapes of varying colours such as a purple triangle, a navy star and so on.

- Auditory

  - Imagine the sound of a bell, a cat purring, rain on the window, a clock ticking.

- Tactile

  - Imagine stroking a cat or a dog or a piece of velvet material.

  - Imagine holding a ball of rubber bands or an orange in your hand.

- Taste and smell

  - Imagine eating a piece of soft fruit, chewing a toffee or drinking hot chocolate.

  - Imagine the smell of the sea, the smell of a bakery or the smell of a flower.

Expansion ideas

What did you notice about your body?

How easy or difficult did you find this exercise? Why do you think that?

How easy or difficult was it for you to focus on one image or one part of your body? Were some images easier to focus on than others?

What did you do or what did you say to yourself when you noticed that you were thinking about something else? How successful was this in helping you to focus back on your body/the image again?

Notes

Additional notes and reflections

Concentrating for Longer Periods

Keep it going

⑦   ☑ self-confidence (E)

⏱ 10 minutes   ☑ effective observation (A)

🕴 🕴   ☑ flexibility of thought (S)

💬

The basic game   Players sit or stand behind each other in a line. The first player taps the second player on the shoulder. This person turns to face the first player who then mimes a short sequence such as planting a seed in a pot and watering it, or cutting a slice of bread and spreading butter on it. The second player has to remember the sequence to show to the third player and so on. The final player tries to guess what the first player was actually miming.

Adaptations   The sequence can be made longer and more complicated or simplified to include just two parts.

Players work in pairs and pass on sequences of gestures that involve two people cooperating (e.g. folding up a parachute and putting it away).

Expansion ideas   Did the sequence change as it was passed around the group? Why did this happen?

What did you do after you had taken your turn to pass on the mime?

Was it easy or difficult to keep concentrating on the game? Why was this?

What helps you to concentrate?

What sort of things make it harder for you to concentrate?

Notes

Our story

⑤   ☑ self-confidence (E)

🕐 5 minutes   ☑ adaptability (A)

👤 👤   ☑ shifting attention (S)

💬

This is a variation of a popular game called 'the old family coach'.

The basic game   The game coordinator makes up a short story about the group, using each player's name at least three times. When a player hears her own name she stands up, turns round three times and takes a bow! When the game coordinator says 'all the children' or 'everyone', the whole group stands up, turns round three times and takes a bow.

For example: 'The new classroom was ready at last and *all the children* waited excitedly in the playground on the first day of term. The head teacher asked *Edward* and *Jodie* to fetch the registers from the office. On the way inside they bumped into *Karen* and *Amarjeet* who had gone to fetch the school bell. *Sam* was allowed to ring the bell and he rang it so loudly that *Marcus* and *Sandeep* put their hands over their ears. Then *Edward* and *Michèle* led *everyone* into their new classroom...' and so on.

Adaptations   Make the story complex, exciting or scary so that players need to swap between being absorbed in the story and listening for their names.

Use a response that requires only slight or no physical movement.

Use musical instruments for players to signal when they hear their name.

Base the story on an imaginary situation where things went wrong because no one was listening and the children had to put everything right.

Expansion ideas   Saying someone's name is a good way to get her attention. What else is it OK to do when we want to say something to someone who doesn't seem to be listening? What is it *not* OK to do?

What do you feel if you don't hear something important?

Is it easy or difficult to focus on one thing (e.g. names) when you are listening to a story? Why is this?

Is it usually easy or difficult for you to hear instructions when you are trying to solve a problem? Why is this?

What would make this game easier? What would make it harder?

Notes

The good news and the bad news

⑦   ☑ self-confidence (E)

🕐 5 minutes   ☑ imagination (A)

🕴 🕴 🕴   ☑ flexibility of thought (S)

💬💬💬

The basic game	Players sit in a circle. The game coordinator starts off with a piece of 'good' news. The next person adds 'but the bad news is...' For example: 'The good news is that school is closed for the day...but the bad news is that we all have extra homework to do. The good news is that the homework is to write about the local funfair...but the bad news is that the funfair is closed for repairs... The good news is that the owner of the funfair is giving away free ice cream...but the bad news is they don't have any cones.'
Adaptations	Play this in pairs with a strict time limit.
	Keep the good and bad news related to a single theme such as the weather or bathing the dog.
Expansion ideas	Was it easier to think up good news or bad news? Why was that?
	Is this easier to do in pairs or in a big group? Why is that?
	Have you ever been in a difficult situation that turned out to be useful for you?
	Can you remember how the story started off?
Notes	

Magic threes

⑦   ☑ self-knowledge (E)

⏱ 10 minutes   ☑ imagination (A)

♦ ♦   ☑ memory strategies (S)

💭💭💭

The basic game	Players have three minutes to walk around the room and introduce themselves to three other people. Each child tells these three people three important facts about herself. For younger children this could be full name, something I hate and something I like. For older children this could be my greatest achievement, my best birthday and my most treasured possession, or one thing that makes me angry, one thing I do to chill out and one thing I want to achieve.
	When the time is up, everyone sits in a circle and recounts as much information about as many other children as possible.
Adaptations	Pairs share the information and then introduce each other to the rest of the group.
	Players divide into groups of three or four and try to find three things that they all have in common. One person from each small group tells the whole group what these three things were.
Expansion ideas	How difficult or easy was it to remember what you heard? Why was this? What would make it easier/harder to remember facts about other people?
	Does the ability to remember things help you to concentrate? Why do you think this?
	Is it better to ask three questions all at once or to ask them one at a time? How long can you comfortably wait in order to give the other person time to think of her answer?
	Why is it important to remember what people tell us about themselves? What does it feel like when someone remembers something important about you? What does it feel like when people get the facts wrong?
Notes	

The rule of the realm

⑦

🕐 10 minutes

♦ ♦ ♦

💬💬💬

☑ self and others (E)

☑ effective observation (A)

☑ problem solving (S)

The basic game

Divide the group into two. Group A leaves the room. Group B makes up a 'talking rule' such as 'Every time you speak you must cross your arms' or 'Every time you finish speaking you must scratch your head'. The game coordinator checks that everyone in Group B remembers to do this by asking each one a simple question such as 'Do you like chocolate?' or 'How old are you?' Group A returns to the room and the coordinator repeats the previous questions or asks similar ones while group A observes. The aim is for group A to guess the rule. The emphasis is on group problem solving – if one person in group A guesses the correct rule, this means that the whole group has achieved. Older children can therefore be encouraged to confer before they guess the rule.

Adaptations

Allow a maximum of five guesses.

Rules for older and very able children can be quite complex such as 'When the coordinator asks you a question, it is the person on your left who answers' or 'You have to use the last word from the question to start your answer'.

The whole group stays in the room and the coordinator chooses a place to set up her kingdom (e.g. the moon, the playground). Players say what they will bring if they are chosen to be part of the new kingdom. The rule that they have to discover relates either to the first letter of their own name or to the first letter of the place where the kingdom will be. The coordinator starts by giving a few examples such as 'Sandip would be welcome in the new kingdom if he brought *s*nakes with him but not if he brought *m*oney. *M*iriam would be welcome if she brought *m*oney, but definitely not if she brought *j*ewels'. The coordinator tells group members if they can join the kingdom or not according to what they offer to bring with them. This needs a strict time limit and therefore clues may need to be made more and more obvious to give everyone the chance to guess the rule and join the kingdom. Players should be encouraged to help each other by giving clues in order to ensure that no one is left out.

Expansion ideas Do all groups need rules? Why/why not? Are some rules more useful than others?

What does it feel like to not know a group rule when it seems as if everyone else knows it? What should groups do about that?

Do different groups have different rules? Why is that?

What do you think about having rules for listening or rules for sitting still? When might such rules be useful? When might they not be useful?

Notes

Who walked past?

⑦   ☑ self-confidence (E)

🕐 10 minutes   ☑ effective listening (A)

🚶 🚶 🚶   ☑ deduction (S)

💬💬

This is based on a game from Singapore (Dunn 1978, pp.59–61).

The basic game

Player A is the catcher. Player B is the caller. All other players stand to one side of Player B. The catcher is blindfolded. She sits on the floor with the caller standing behind her. The caller calls out a character or animal – for example, 'an old man walking with a stick' or 'a dog chasing a cat'. She then points to one of the players near her who has to walk past the catcher acting the part. The caller continues to call out different characters or animals until all the players have had a turn. The catcher then removes the blindfold. The caller names one of the characters and the catcher tries to guess who played the part. The catcher is allowed three guesses. If she guesses correctly, she changes places with that child who then becomes the catcher. If she does not guess correctly after three attempts, she plays the catcher for a second time. The caller also changes places with another player after each round.

Adaptations

Think up a list of possible characters before starting the game.

Use appropriate props (e.g. a walking stick) to increase the complexity of the characteristics that the catcher is listening out for.

Expansion ideas

Was it easy or difficult to recognise the players? Why was this?

What sort of things were you listening for to help you to identify the players?

Players need to use their imaginations to think about being different characters. Why is this an important ability?

Notes

Abandon ship!

⑨   ☑ self-confidence (E)

🕐 30 minutes   ☑ adaptability (A)

🚶 🚶 🚶   ☑ negotiation (S)

💬💬💬

The basic game   Split into pairs or small groups of equal numbers, according to the size of the whole group. Within each group, members imagine that they are on a boat that is about to sink. They have a lifeboat but they are only allowed to take ten items with them from the ship. First, they think of ten items each. They then have to negotiate with other team members as to what to take because they can only take ten items between them. Groups then join with another group and renegotiate the ten items. Eventually, the whole group meets and negotiates a final ten items.

Adaptation   The whole group has been shipwrecked. They have two empty plastic bottles to use on the desert island. Small groups or pairs think of as many uses as possible for the two bottles. The whole group then pools their ideas.

Expansion ideas   How did this feel? Is everyone happy with the final decision? Is everyone happy with how the negotiations went?

Did everyone get a chance to put their ideas forward? In the final group, did a clear leader emerge?

How easy or difficult was it to agree on ten items?

For this game, players need to be imaginative and they need to focus and concentrate on the task. Can you think of some real situations when you have used these abilities and skills?

Notes

Additional notes and reflections

11

Self-Calming

Sleeping giants

⑤   ☑ self-reliance (E)

🕐 5 minutes   ☑ self-control (A)

👤 👤 👤   ☑ monitoring breathing (S)

💬

The basic game   Players pretend to be giants. They stamp around the room with heavy footsteps until the game coordinator gives a signal, such as ringing a small bell or raising one hand in the air. Then the giants lie down on the ground and close their eyes. The game coordinator walks quietly around the room to see if they are all 'asleep'. The coordinator can talk but must not touch the giants. If any giants are seen to move, then they must sit up and keep looking for any others who are moving.

Adaptations   Use two different types of music – one very loud with a heavy beat and one quiet and gentle. The giants move to the sound of the first and lie down when they hear the second; or they move more slowly to the gentle music and lie down when the music stops.

Finish the game with a calm period when everyone is lying down or sitting quietly, listening to calm music or listening to a short story.

Expansion ideas   How easy or difficult is it for you to stay still and calm?

How easy or difficult is it for you to be active and to listen or watch for a signal from someone else?

When the giants were stamping around, did anyone bump into another giant? Why do you think this happened?

Does your breathing change when you are being calm? How does it change? When might it be useful to make your breathing calm on purpose?

Notes

Guess how!

⑦   ☑ self-awareness (E)

⏱ 10 minutes   ☑ effective observation (A)

👤 👤 👤   ☑ self-rewarding (S)

💬

The basic game   Two players leave the room while everyone else decides what
                  'angry position' or 'calm position' they should take up on their
                  return. For anger, this might be something like 'sitting on the
                  floor, facing away from each other with arms and legs folded'.
                  The two players return and try to work out how they should be
                  sitting or standing according to how loudly or quietly the rest of
                  the group are clapping. The closer they get to the target position,
                  the louder everyone else claps.

Adaptation   The two players who left the room return and 'arrange' two other
                  players in pre-chosen positions.

Expansion ideas   Sometimes we get feedback from others about whether or not
                  we're succeeding in a task or if we're 'on the right track', but
                  sometimes we have to rely on our own self-awareness.

                  Talk about being realistic in self-awareness. How do you know
                  when you are doing something well? How do you know when
                  you are tense or when you are relaxed?

                  How do you know when you need to do something in a different
                  way?

Notes

Puppets

⑤

🕐 5 minutes

♦ ♦ ♦

💬

☑ self-awareness (E)

☑ self-control (A)

☑ monitoring physical sensations (S)

The basic game

Players pretend to be puppets. They start in a standing position with their feet firmly on the ground, their arms stretched upwards and fingers spread out as though they are being held up by strings. They imagine that the strings are very slowly being loosened so that their body starts to drop down. Start with just the fingers, then hands, arms, head and upper body, finally bending slightly at the knees. The same movements are then performed in reverse until all players are standing upright again with arms stretched as high as they can. Do this several times at varying speeds. End with a shake to relax arms and legs again.

Adaptations

Make puppet movements in time to different types and speeds of music.

In pairs, take turns at being puppet and puppeteer. Without touching the puppet, the puppeteer pretends to pull strings to get different parts of the puppet to move in different directions and at different speeds. This works well if the puppet is lying down to start with and the puppeteer has to work out which strings to pull in order to get the puppet to stand up.

Alternate between being a rag doll and a wooden or metal toy.

Expansion ideas

What does it feel like to have a relaxed body? How does that compare with being tense?

What aspects of movement can you control (e.g. speed, direction)?

Is it possible to control our own thinking? When might it be easy to do this? When might it be difficult?

Think about the complicated sequence of movements needed to stand up or sit down. How do we learn how to do this?

When are you most relaxed?

What sorts of things help you to feel relaxed?

What might make you feel tense?

Can you tell when your muscles are relaxed and when they are tense? Do you ever think about your shoulders, your back, the backs of your knees?

How did the puppet and the puppeteer cooperate? What did you each need to do? How easy or difficult was this? Which role did you enjoy the most?

Notes

Imagine this: Feeling tense and feeling relaxed

⑦

🕐 10 minutes

🚶 🚶

💬

☑ self-reliance (E)

☑ imagination (A)

☑ choosing strategies (S)

The basic activity Read the following slowly and calmly, giving children plenty of time to follow your instructions.

> Let's think about what our bodies feel like when we have different emotions.
>
> Think of a time when you felt a bit upset or cross about something. I bet your body felt very stiff and perhaps you felt a bit churned up inside? This is called tension.
>
> If tension was an animal or a plant or anything else, what would it be? …
>
> Close your eyes and imagine something that somehow shows us what it's like to be tense…
>
> Imagine that you can become your image of tension… Step into being this plant or animal or object… What do you feel like when you are this image?
>
> What does your body feel like? … What is the worst thing about being this image? … Feel a frown growing from deep inside you… Feel it spreading all the way through you… Really notice what this is like…
>
> Now step out of being this image and back to being you… Give yourself a shake all over… Shake your hands, shake your arms, shake your body, shake your legs! Let all that tension disappear…
>
> Draw or write about your image of tension on a big piece of paper. When you have finished, we'll do the next bit of imagining…
>
> When we are not tense, our body feels more relaxed.

If the feeling of relaxing was an animal, a plant or an object, what would it be?

Close your eyes and take three deep breaths, letting the air out slowly as you breathe out... Ask your imagination to come up with an image that somehow shows us what it's like to be relaxed... It could be an object, a plant or an animal... Whatever it is, just let the image appear...

When you are ready, imagine that you can become your image of relaxation...

Step into being this animal or plant or object and really feel what it's like...

What does your body feel like? ...

Feel a smile grow from deep inside you... Feel it spreading all the way through you... Really notice what this is like...

What is the best thing about being this image? ...

Spend some time just being this image and enjoying the feelings... When you are ready, step out of this image and back to being you. Open your eyes slowly and have a stretch and a yawn!

On a large piece of paper, draw or write about your feelings of being relaxed.

Expansion ideas Talk about the different physical sensations that we produce in our body when we are relaxed.

What does it feel like to be tense and what does it feel like to be very relaxed? Notice the difference between being very tense and feeling strong without feeling excessive tension.

Why is it important for our bodies to be relaxed sometimes? (To help us to feel calm, emotion regulation, feeling of well-being, concentration, better sleep.)

Is there such a thing as useful tension? When do we need to be tense?

Are there times when you have tension in your body that doesn't need to be there?

Invite the children to contribute to a list of 'ways to look after myself'. This list might include such things as going for a walk, relaxing in a deep bath, having a 'quiet time', playing with my dog/cat, having a hug, etc. Try to get at least 20 items on the list. Each child can then decide on up to three things that they will do when they are feeling worried, fed-up or tired during the next week. Be specific. For example, 'When I notice signs of stress/ when I notice myself getting uptight/I will go for a ten minute walk/relax on my bed/take some time for myself/play with the dog/talk to a friend.'

For this activity, players needed to use their imagination. How could you use your imagination in the future to help you to feel calm?

Notes

Mindfulness of breathing

⑤   ☑ self-acceptance (E)

🕐 5 minutes   ☑ self-control (A)

♦ ♦ ♦   ☑ monitoring internal 'chatter' (S)

💬

The basic activity   Everyone sits in a circle. They place one hand lightly on their chest and the other hand just below their bottom ribs. Instruct everyone to take a full breath in through their nose while you count to four, gently pause for the count of two and then breathe out gradually through their mouth while they notice what happens to their hands.

Ideally, each child will have felt his stomach move downwards and outwards when he breathed in. There will have been only slight movement in his chest. His shoulders will have hardly moved at all and his posture will have remained balanced. This is diaphragmatic breathing. If a child raised his shoulders and expanded his chest or pulled in his stomach as he took a full breath, he was not breathing in a relaxed way. Diaphragmatic breathing is very natural but may take a while to relearn if a child's breathing pattern has changed over the years.

Once children have got the basic idea of relaxed breathing, read the following instructions to them:

> Now gently close your eyes…and put all your attention into your breathing. Just noticing it without trying to change anything… Notice the feel of the air as you breathe in and the feel of the air as you breathe out… Keep noticing your breathing… When you have other thoughts, just let them float through your mind and then go back to noticing your breathing again… We are going to carry on doing this for a little while…just sitting quietly, noticing how we breathe [*do this for one minute*]… Now you are ready to gradually open your eyes and…[*move the children gently on to the next task*].

Adaptations   Gradually increase the length of time that the children sit like this. A good guide is to work towards one minute for each year of age.

Breathe in for the count of four. Gently hold the breath for the count of two and then breathe out for the count of four. Do this together with one other person. Now see if you can keep doing this while carrying out a simple task such as putting away some pencils together or walking around the room together.

Expansion ideas   How do you feel when your breathing is calm?

When might you need to have faster breathing?

How easy or difficult was it for you to just notice your breathing? Why was that? Did you notice other thoughts come into your mind when you were sitting quietly? It would be very hard to stop these thoughts, but it is good to notice when they come and then just let them go and return your attention to your breathing.

Once children are able to direct their attention to the diaphragm, they will notice themselves taking relaxing deep breaths during the day and this will help them to feel calm. Suggest to the children that they can also consciously take two or three relaxed breaths to help control any feelings of anxiety before these get too big.

Notes

Toning

---

⑦

🕐 15 minutes

♦ ♦ ♦

💬

☑ self-reliance (E)

☑ self-control (A)

☑ pausing and refocusing (S)

Children will need to do the 'Mindfulness of breathing' activity, p.121 before doing this activity so that they are not forcing their breath.

The basic activity   Read the following instructions with plenty of pauses to allow time for children to absorb the information.

> We're going to do something that's called toning. For this we need to have our backs as straight as possible [*the best position is to be seated cross-legged on the floor*] so that we are perfectly balanced and relaxed. Relax your shoulders. Put one hand on your tummy and feel what happens when you breathe. As you take a breath in, feel the air go all the way down into your lungs. Because your lungs need room to fill up with air, your tummy will come outwards; your shoulders will hardly move at all. Most people get this the wrong way round to start with! When you breathe out, your tummy will move inwards [*allow a few moments for everyone to get the idea of this way of breathing*]. Now forget about your breathing for a while. Just let the air go in and out without thinking about it while I tell you about toning.
>
>   When we make different sounds with our voices, this can help us to feel refreshed and well. Everyone can do toning even if they think they can't sing very well. It's fun and it's easy to do. When we make certain sounds, we can make different parts of our body vibrate or shake a little bit. Your voice comes when you vibrate the tiny muscles inside your throat. I'll show you what I mean. Place three fingers of one hand over your throat just where your Adam's apple is. Let them rest there gently. Now take a breath and let it out while you are humming…did you feel your throat vibrate? Try that again… Now place your hands along the length of both sides of your nose. Hum gently and notice what you can feel… Can you feel the vibrations inside your nose? … When we tone and when we sing, we are making

our bodies vibrate all the time. All the tiniest bits of us are moving, jiggling around and helping us to feel good!

Now let's try a bit of proper toning. Begin by breathing in through your nose. Feel the air going right down to the bottom of your lungs and feel first your tummy and then your chest moving outwards. Now let the air go as you say the sound 'UH' as in 'huh'. This is a very deep sound but it doesn't have to be loud. Say it very gently and make it last as long as you can without running out of breath. In a moment we'll do that one again together. While you tone the sound, this time close your eyes and try to think of the colour red. It might help to think of a big red flower or a red blanket. Try to make the sound last for as long as possible but stop before you begin to force your breath out. [*Make this sound three times in all.*]

Now we're going to do the same with the sound 'OOO' as in 'two'. This sound is not quite as deep as the 'UH'. We need to make our voices a little bit higher and, this time, we'll think of the colour orange. What could we have that would help us to think of orange? [*Make the sound 'OOO' three times as before.*]

The next sound is 'OH' as in the word 'low'. It's a little bit higher than 'OOO' and the colour we're going to think of is yellow. Can you think of something nice that will help us to see yellow? [*Make the sound three times, remembering to keep the sounds long and gentle.*]

Now we're going to make the sound 'AH' as in the word 'park'. While we're doing this, we'll try to think of the colour green. What will help you to think of this colour? The sound needs to be a little higher than 'OH'. We have to make our voices go up a bit as though we are singing a higher note. [*Make this sound three times.*]

The next sound is 'EYE' as in the word 'my' and the colour that goes with this one is blue. What would you like to think of for blue? Begin to tone this sound a little higher than the last one. [*Make this sound three times again.*]

Now we're going to move up to the sound 'AYE' as in the word 'may'. The colour that goes with this is a very deep blue (indigo). Can you think of something that's got that colour in it? [*Repeat the sound as before.*]

The last sound is 'EEE' as in 'me'. This is the very highest sound we are going to make. Imagine this sound making the very top of your head vibrate while you think of the colour violet. [*Tone this sound three times. Because of the shift in energies that this toning produces, you or the children may feel a little light-headed. You can sit and just enjoy this feeling for a while if you like, but when you are ready to feel a bit more 'grounded', just tone 'UH' again three times.*]

What are you feeling now? ... I'm feeling [*say how you feel*].

Adaptations
Tone the sounds while focusing on different areas of the body for each tone and 'sense' that area vibrating. The following sequence for toning is that suggested by Jonathan Goldman (1995):

'UH' located at the base of the spine

'OOO' located about three inches below the naval

'OH' extending from the navel several inches upwards (to the solar plexus)

'AH' centred in the middle of the chest, near to the heart

'EYE' located at the throat

'AYE' centred in the forehead between and slightly above the eyes.

'EEE' located at the top of the head.

Note what each of you felt like before you started this exercise and what each of you feels like at the end of it. Remember, if you feel slightly light-headed, tone 'UH' again a few times at the end.

Expansion ideas
How easy or difficult was it for you to focus on different colours or different parts of your body while you were toning? Why do you think this?

Do you ever notice yourself looking at something or listening to something while thinking about something completely different?

Can you listen, look and 'do' all at the same time? What might make this easier? What might make it harder?

How did you feel when you had finished this exercise?

For this activity, players needed to use their imaginations. How can this activity help you to feel calm and focused in the future?

Notes

Musical drawing

⑤

⊕ 15 minutes

♦ ♦ ♦

☐

☑ self-expression (E)

☑ imagination (A)

☑ controlling focus of attention (S)

The basic game   The game coordinator plays a variety of music and the group draws whatever comes to mind while listening to the different rhythms and moods.

Adaptation   Children bring in their own selections of music and talk about how they feel when they listen to it.

Expansion ideas   Does listening to music affect how you are feeling? Is there a piece of music that always makes you feel sad or always makes you feel happy? Why do you think this is?

Are other members of the group affected in the same way by the same piece of music? Why do you think this is?

Are you able to imagine a piece of music without actually hearing it?

How can you use the images that you drew to help you to feel calm, happy, in control, etc. in the future?

Notes

Fidget flop

⑤   ☑ self-reliance (E)

🕑 5 minutes   ☑ self-control (A)

♦ ♦ ♦   ☑ choosing strategies (S)

💬

This can be done at any time as a brief way to release tension and is useful prior to an activity that requires a lot of concentration. Read the instructions slowly, allowing as much time as feels comfortable for children to 'play' with the movements.

The basic activity   Imagine that your fingers are all animals or people and they're having a pretend play-fight. Make them play at fighting each other. Get them tangled up and then untangle them again... Now let them slowly stop...and then make them float instead. Let your fingers float around each other without touching...and now gently stroke your fingers across each other... Now have them fight each other again. They're moving faster and faster... Gradually they slow down... Can you feel them tingling? Let your fingers gently float around each other again... Now let your hands flop down as though they've gone to sleep.

Adaptation   Children imagine that they are holding a soft ball in both hands. They can squeeze the ball tightly and then let it expand again, or squeeze and mould an imaginary ball of clay.

Expansion ideas   Do you ever do things that help you to get ready to concentrate? What helps? Why does this help?

Do you concentrate better when you are tense or when you are relaxed? (Or does it depend on what you are doing?) Why do you think this?

Notes

Peer massage

⑤   ☑ self and others (E)

🕐 10 minutes   ☑ adaptability (A)

👤 👤 👤   ☑ empathy (S)

💬

The basic game   Players sit in a circle with their backs to each other. Each player asks the person in front of him for permission to give him a massage. Players silently massage each other's back, neck and shoulders for two minutes. When the time is up, everyone thanks the person who gave them a massage.

Adaptations   Players offer each other a back and shoulder massage in pairs. This helps the giver and receiver to really concentrate on what is happening. The receiver can ask his partner to alter the massage – for example, by going more gently or more slowly.

Players take turns to close their eyes while their partner slowly draws a shape (circle, square, triangle) or writes a word on their palm with one finger. The person with his eyes closed has to guess the shape or word. He can ask for up to three repetitions if it is hard to guess. If he gets it right, they swap places.

In pairs, players take turns to 'drum' on each other's back (very gently) with their fingertips. They finish by laying their palms on their partner's back and resting them there quietly for 30 seconds.

Players give themselves an imaginary shampoo, using fingertips to massage their own heads.

One player sits facing away from the group. Everyone takes turns to spell out their name in large letters on this person's back. If the first player guesses the name correctly, the two swap places.

Expansion ideas   How do you feel after this game?

How does this game help us with other activities?

Which is most sensitive to touch, your back or your fingertips?

Are you aware of sensations all the time? For example, do you notice your sleeves against your arms all day?

Why is it important to be able to change the focus of our attention from one sensation to another or from one task or object to another?

Is it possible to pay attention to two different senses or two different tasks at once?

Notes

Getting ready for listening

⑤   ☑ self-reliance (E)

🕐 2 minutes   ☑ imagination (A)

♦ ♦ ♦   ☑ choosing strategies (S)

💬

The basic activity   Read the following instructions slowly with plenty of pauses.

It's nice to rest quietly sometimes and to listen with the whole of our body, not just our ears. Let's see where our listening takes us today. Gently close your eyes and feel yourself relaxing all over so that every bit of you feels heavy and loose. When you breathe in, you can feel a lovely warmth filling up your body. Each time you breathe out you are breathing away all the tightness in your muscles that you don't need when you are just listening. Feel the air as it very slowly goes in and out of you… Imagine that there is a yellow light which is coming up from beneath your feet. It moves through your feet…your legs…your body…your arms…your shoulders… and your head…and it goes through the top of your head and floats away…so now you feel very relaxed but still wide awake and able to listen with every little part of you.

Adaptation   Encourage children to choose their own colour for relaxation.

Expansion ideas   Instead of a colour, what else could you imagine that would help you to feel relaxed but 'alert' and ready to listen?

Do you always need to feel relaxed in order to listen? Why do you think this?

Notes

Just hanging loose

⑦

🕐 10 minutes

♦ ♦ ♦

💬

☑ self-awareness (E)

☑ self-control (A)

☑ monitoring physical sensations (S)

The basic activity   Find a really comfortable position to sit [*lie*] in, ready to let your whole body go loose... Let your body sink into the chair or cushion [*bed*] so that now you are as still as can be... Begin to think about your toes. Relax your toes and feel them getting warm and heavy... Let all the tightness just float away from your toe muscles so that they are not having to do any extra work... Now let go of any tightness in your legs. Put all your attention into your legs and let the muscles relax, release, let go.

When your legs are relaxed, begin to think about your tummy. Feel the muscles in your tummy go soft, relaxing and releasing any tightness that might have been there... Feel your hands and arms getting warm and heavy as they rest comfortably by your sides... Your fingers are very slightly curled but there is no tightness in them...

Now think about your shoulders. Gently raise your shoulders up towards your ears now and feel how the muscles have to work to keep them there... Then let go...and feel the difference... Notice how it felt when they were tight and how it feels when your shoulders are more relaxed... Now let go even more than you thought you could...

Think about your face. Feel a smile starting to come... Let the smile spread and spread until it reaches your eyes... Now let go so that all the muscles on your face gently relax and your forehead feels a little wider and higher than it did before... If you haven't already shut your eyes, let your eyelids gently close now... Feel them become heavier and heavier so that you couldn't open them even if you tried... Notice your breathing. Be very still as you feel the air going into your body when you breathe gently and quietly... Feel it as it slowly goes out again... In and out like waves on the seashore... In...and...out... In...and...out...

Now forget about your breathing and just feel yourself relaxing more and more... Stay like this for a little while and imagine a special place where you like to be...

[*Allow the group to rest for 2–3 minutes.*]

Now you are going to let the image of your favourite place begin to fade... You are becoming more aware of this room that we're in and the people around you... Open your eyes...your body is still relaxed but your mind is awake and ready to [*do whatever you have planned for the next activity*].

Adaptation	Instead of imagining a special place, continue with a short story.
Expansion ideas	Make a list of different ways that we can relax our bodies and our minds.
	Talk about mental and emotional busyness as well as physical busyness.
Notes	

Additional notes and reflections

12

Celebrating

The three activities in this session are primarily for seven-year-olds and above, but shortened versions can be used with children as young as five. These activities offer a way of drawing together the abilities and skills necessary for focusing, concentrating and self-calming and help children to acknowledge and celebrate their achievements.

Pass a gift

⑦   ☑ self-acceptance (E)

⏱ 10 minutes   ☑ imagination (A)

🛉 🛉 🛉   ☑ joint attention (S)

💬

The basic activity Use a large glitter ball or a beautiful/unusual object. Pass the ball to each other around the group. Whoever is holding it praises someone else and passes her the ball. This is best done in sequence around the circle to start with until you feel that children can praise each other in random order and not leave anyone out. Encourage children to say 'thank you' when praised or to give a non-verbal acknowledgement of the praise.

Adaptations   Brainstorm praises before you start.

Let children take turns in choosing the object to be used.

Choose different methods of praising on different occasions or for different levels of ability (see notes on praising in Chapter 4).

Expansion ideas   What do you feel when you give and receive praise?

How many different ways can we praise each other?

What would you most like to be praised for? What do you think your mother/brother/best friend would most like to be praised for?

Is there anything you *don't* like to be praised for?

How do you praise yourself?

Notes

Spaceship to the stars

⑦   ☑ self-confidence (E)

🕐 15 minutes   ☑ imagination (A)

❗ ❗ ❗   ☑ setting goals (S)

💬

This activity is adapted from an original exercise by Dina Glouberman (1992, p.187). Projecting yourself into the future to imagine how things will turn out is a powerful aid to making changes. Such imagery requires the suspending of judgement and reality in order to act 'as if' you had already achieved your desired outcome.

The basic activity This imagework exercise will be most effective if each child has a particular goal in mind before starting.

Just the right star

Find a comfortable position...and gently let your eyes close. Take three full breaths, breathing in right down into the bottom of your lungs and breathing out slowly and calmly.

Let's imagine that you can travel into the future in your own special spaceship. Imagine what that spaceship looks like... What colour is it? ... What shape?

Notice what it sounds like. Can you see the spaceship door?... If you go inside you will see a really comfortable chair to sit in with some controls on a board in front of it and a large window that goes at least halfway around the ship.

Imagine yourself sitting at the controls. There are lots of them. There's a button that has a sign under it saying 'to the stars' and one that says 'back home'. When you're ready to go, all you have to do is press the button for the stars and the spaceship will gently take off and head up into the sky. You will be totally in control. Ready? ... You're climbing high up into the sky now... You are travelling through the clouds. The sky around you is becoming a deeper and deeper blue and you can see the stars shining ahead of you. You're going high into the place where everything and anything is possible...

Somewhere up here is your own special star... Search around for a little while until you can see it clearly in front of you... Have you found it? ... Notice all the little details about this very special star as the spaceship hovers near it and circles around it... If there is something you have to get done or a goal you want to set for yourself, then this star will be able to show you what things will be like for you once you've achieved it. If you've thought of something, you can try it out now or, if not, you can come back again another time. Tell me if there is something you'd like to be able to do...

Now, imagine that there is a beam of light shining out from the star into the sky. It can project pictures on to the sky as though you were at the cinema. As you watch, you can see a big screen forming in the sky ahead of you. On to this screen walks a person... it's you! This is you after you've achieved your goal. What do you look like on the screen? ... What is the future 'you' doing now? ... What did you do to make this happen? ... What did you need to have or to know so that you could achieve your goal? ... How is 'you' on the screen different from 'you' sitting in the spaceship? ... If the future 'you' could whisper something special to you in the spaceship, what would they whisper? ... The future 'you' says goodbye and is walking away now. As you watch, the beam of light from the star starts to get fainter and the screen starts to fade until eventually it has disappeared all together... How are you feeling now?

Time now to leave the stars. Take one last look around... Press the button that says 'back home' and away goes the spaceship, through the deep blue sky...through the floating clouds...slowly and gently back down to earth. . .

As you get out of the spaceship, notice if you feel any different now to how you felt when you first set off... Now you're walking away from the spaceship. Feel yourself coming back to the room... Notice the feel of your body... Listen to the sounds around you... Keep your eyes closed for a little while longer while you have a little stretch... When you are ready, open your eyes and look around you... Stamp your feet on the floor a bit to bring you properly back down to earth!

Notes

Confidence Groups

⑦

🕐 15 minutes

☑ self-confidence (E)

☑ imagination (A)

☑ giving and receiving praise (S)

The idea for these groups is based on the format for oekos or 'home' groups, which are an established element of imagework training, combined with aspects of techniques developed by Lee Glickstein (1998) as a means of personal development in public speaking. Glickstein's work is well known in the UK as a self-help tool for adults who stutter. Specialist speech and language therapists Carolyn Desforges and Louise Tonkinson (2006) have also developed a particular version of his approach which they use with children. With their kind permission, I have taken some of the principles that they outline and have altered the format to create 'Confidence Groups'. These groups aim to emphasise and promote existing skills as well as developing new skills. They promote connectedness with peers in a very meaningful way – giving children a forum in which to be heard and accepted by their peers and giving them the opportunity to learn how to receive acceptance and 'positive regard' from others.

My own experience of using this format is that it has proved to be an invaluable tool – the children love doing it and the respect and empathy generated between children has a marked effect in other situations. Their ability to self-monitor and self-evaluate in a realistic way is enhanced and the positive feedback from peers is a major boost to self-esteem. Of course, once demonstrated and practised, the principles of focusing on foundation elements, abilities and skills, connecting with others in order to really 'receive' praise and respect, and the giving of positive, specific feedback can all be generalised for use in situations other than a planned Confidence Group.

Format for
'Confidence
Groups'

Where you are working with large numbers of children (e.g. a class), this works best if you split into smaller groups. I have facilitated 'Confidence Groups' with up to 12 children participating, but obviously the size of the group depends partly on the length of time available and the number of facilitators/helpers who know the format.

Stage one

For these groups to work there are three principles which need to be established with the children from the outset:

1. *Focus on the positive.* When children take part in the group, whether giving or receiving feedback, they are reminded and encouraged to focus on skills not deficits.

2. *The group members offer support to the speaker.* This is discussed with the children in terms of what 'support' means and how we show support and acceptance of others, particularly how we show acceptance non-verbally by fully listening.

3. *The speaker 'connects' with the audience.* This is established by helping children to focus on eye contact and breathing calmly. Children are encouraged both to sense the acceptance from their audience and to be aware of physical ways in which this is shown. This may seem a difficult concept for some at first, but they can be reassured that there is no right or wrong way of doing this.

The children sit in a circle and are invited to relax and to 'tune into' themselves ('Notice what your body is feeling... Notice where your thoughts are drifting to... Be aware of the other people in the small group, then tune back into yourself again').

The first round in the group generally doesn't involve any speaking at all. Instead, the children each take a turn to walk up to the 'stage' (an identified space in the circle). They make slow eye contact with each of the group members in the audience and then walk back to their seat. The audience return eye contact and silently 'send' their complete acceptance. The 'speaker' is asked to be open to receive this acceptance. When the children return to their seat, specific, truthful feedback is given by the group facilitators on looking confident, walking in a confident way, using calm breathing to settle themselves, gaining support by using eye contact, etc. The same format can be used with the children remaining seated and taking turns around the circle if this is more appropriate.

Stage two   The children take turns to walk up to the speaker position. They give and receive natural, gentle eye contact to everyone in turn and can then choose whether or not to say one word or a short sentence. They could perhaps introduce themselves or say something that they like, or just say 'Hello' before returning to their chairs. This time, feedback is given primarily from group members, with a small amount of feedback from facilitators. The facilitators then praise the group members for the content and quality of the positive feedback given.

Stage three   The children walk up to the speaker position, take time to settle themselves, look around the audience and then say one or two sentences appropriate to the theme for the day. Once again, the other members of the group simply listen. The speaker is then given feedback by facilitators and group members on particular skills as appropriate. For example, the theme might be 'things I have enjoyed doing' or 'what I did yesterday'. Children are encouraged to give very specific, positive feedback about *what the speaker has just done* such as 'You smiled when you told us that and you looked as though you felt really good about your success', 'You were very brave to go first and speak in front of the whole group' or 'You kept really good eye contact when you said that'.

Of course, this sort of descriptive feedback will come from adult facilitators to start with in order to give an appropriate model, but if you encourage this as a regular feature of groups, children will quickly recognise all the different things they can praise.

Facilitators continue to praise group members for their positive feedback ('You picked up on a very important point in your feedback', 'You are really noticing how people show their feelings', etc.).

Stage four   Gradually increase the time for each person to speak when this feels right, but maximum time should be around two minutes. Keep an eye on the time to ensure that everyone gets an equal turn.

Notes

Bibliography

Arnold, A. (1976) *The World Book of Children's Games*. London: Pan Books.

Bandura, A. (1977) 'Self-efficacy: Towards a unifying theory of behavioural change.' *Psychological Review 84*, 191–215.

Bandura, A. (1989) 'Perceived self-efficacy in the exercise of personal agency.' *The Psychologist: Bulletin of the British Psychological Society 2*, 411–424.

Beswick, C. (2003) *The Little Book of Parachute Play*. Husbands Bosworth: Featherstone Education.

Brandes, D. and Phillips, H. (1979) *Gamesters' Handbook: 140 Games for Teachers and Group Leaders*. London: Hutchinson.

Bruner, J.S., Jolly, A. and Sylva, K. (eds) (1976) *Play: Its Role in Development and Evolution*. Harmondsworth: Penguin.

Carpenter, C.H. (2001) 'Our Dreams in Action: Spirituality and Children's Play Today.' In J.C. Bishop and M. Curtis (eds) *Play Today in the Primary Playground*. Buckingham: Open University Press.

Cohen, D. (1993) *The Development of Play* (2nd edition). London: Routledge.

Dawson, G., Munson, J., Estes, A., Osterling, J. *et al.* (2002) 'Neurocognitive function and joint attention ability in young children with autism spectrum disorder versus developmental delay.' *Child Development 73*, 2, 345–358.

Desforges, C., Tonkinson, L. and Kelly, S. (2006) 'Using the power of speaking circles to develop confident communication.' *Speaking Out*, Spring, 6–7.

Diamond, A. and Lee, K. (2011) 'Interventions shown to aid executive function development in children 4–12 years old.' *Science 333*, 959–64.

Dunn, O. (1978) for the Asian Cultural Centre for UNESCO *Let's Play Asian Games*. Macmillan Southeast Asia in association with the Asian Cultural Centre for UNESCO.

Durham, C. (2006) *Chasing Ideas*. London: Jessica Kingsley Publishers.

Eberle, B. (2008) *Scamper On: More Creative Games and Activities for Imagination Development*. Waco, TX: Prufrock Press.

Eliot, L. (1999) *What's Going on in There? How the Brain and Mind Develop in the First Five Years of Life*. New York, NY: Bantam.

Ellis, M.J. (1973) *Why People Play*. Englewood Cliffs, NJ: Prentice Hall.

Ferrucci, P. (1982) *What We May Be*. London: The Aquarian Press.

Field, T., Lasko, D., Mundy, P., Henteleff, T., Talpins, S. and Dowling, M. (1996) 'Autistic children's attentiveness and responsivity improved after touch therapy.' *Journal of Autism and Developmental Disorders 27*, 329–34.

Fontana, D. and Slack, I. (2007) *Teaching Meditation to Children: The Practical Guide to the Use and Benefits of Meditation Techniques.* London: Watkins Publishing.

Garvey, C. (1977) *Play.* London: Fontana/Open Books.

Gerhardt, S. (2004) *Why Love Matters: How Affection Shapes a Baby's Brain.* London and New York, NY: Routledge.

Glickstein, L. (1998) *Be Heard Now! Tap into Your Inner Speaker and Communicate with Ease.* New York, NY: Broadway Books.

Glosser, G. and Goodglass, H. (1990) 'Disorders in executive control functions among aphasic and other brain damaged patients.' *Journal of Clinical and Experimental Neuropsychology 12,* 485–501.

Glouberman, D. (1992) *Life Choices and Life Changes through Imagework.* London: Aquarian/Thorsons.

Goldman, J. (1995) *Healing Sounds: The Power of Harmonics.* Shaftesbury: Element.

Goleman, D. (1996) *Emotional Intelligence. Why it Can Matter More than IQ.* London: Bloomsbury.

Harter, S. (1999) *The Construction of the Self.* New York, NY: Guilford Press.

Higgins, A.T. and Turnure, J.E. (1984) 'Distractibility and concentration of attention in children's development.' *Child Development 55,* 5, 1799–810.

Kabat-Zinn, J. (1996) *Full Catastrophe Living: How to Cope with Stress, Pain and Illness Using Mindfulness Meditation.* London: Piatkus.

Kaplan, S. (1995) 'The restorative benefits of nature: Toward an integrative framework.' *Journal of Environmental Psychology 15,* 169–82.

Kuo, F.E. and Faber Taylor, A. (2004) 'A potential natural treatment for attentiondeficit/hyperactivity disorder: Evidence from a national study.' *American Journal of Public Health 94,* 9, 1580–86.

Lazar, S.W., Kerr, C.E., Wasserman, R.H., Gray, J.R. *et al.* (2005) 'Meditation experience is associated with increased cortical thickness.' *Neuroreport 16,* 17, 1893–7.

Liebmann, M. (2004) *Art Therapy for Groups: A Handbook of Themes and Exercises* (2nd edition). London and New York, NY: Routledge.

Masheder, M. (1989) *Let's Play Together.* London: Green Print.

Neelands, J. (1990) *Structuring Drama Work: A Handbook of Available Forms in Theatre and Drama.* Cambridge: Cambridge University Press.

Nunn, K., Hanstock, T. and Lask, B. (2008) *Who's Who of the Brain.* London: Jessica Kingsley Publishers.

Olness, K. (1993) 'Self-Regulation and Conditioning.' In B. Moyers (ed.) *Healing and the Mind.* London: Aquarian/Thorsons.

Opie, I. and Opie, P. (1976) 'Street Games: "Counting-out and Chasing".' In J.S. Bruner, A. Jolly and K. Sylva (eds) *Play: Its Role in Development and Evolution.* Harmondsworth: Penguin.

Osborn, A.F. (1993) *Applied Imagination: Principles and Procedures of Creative Problem- Solving* (3rd edition). Creative Education Foundation (original edition 1953).

Paley, V.G. (1991) *The Boy Who Would be a Helicopter.* London: Harvard University Press.

Parrinello, R.M. and Ruff, H.A. (1988) 'The influence of adult intervention on infants' level of attention.' *Child Development 59*, 4, 1125–35.

Plummer, D.M. (2007a) *Helping Children to Build Self-Esteem* (2nd edition). London: Jessica Kingsley Publishers.

Plummer D.M. (2007b) *Self-Esteem Games for Children.* London: Jessica Kingsley Publishers.

Plummer, D.M. (2011) *Helping Children to Improve their Communication Skills.* London: Jessica Kingsley Publishers.

Rinpoche, S. (1995) *The Tibetan Book of Living and Dying.* London: Random House.

Roberts, J.M. and Sutton-Smith, B. (1962) 'Child training and game involvement.' *Ethnology 1*, 166–85.

Rogers, C.R. (1980) *A Way of Being.* Boston, MA: Houghton Mifflin.

Samuels, S.J. and Edwall, G. (1981) 'The role of attention in reading with complications for the learning disabled student.' *Journal of Learning Disabilities 14*, 353–61. Cited in Higgins, A.T. and Turnure, J.E. (1984) 'Distractibility and concentration of attention in children's development.' *Child Development 55*, 5, 1799–810.

Sunderland, M. (2007) *What Every Parent Needs to Know.* London: Dorling Kindersley.

Tart, C.T. (1994) *Living the Mindful Life: a handbook for living in the present moment.* Boston, Massachusetts: Shambhala Publications Inc.

Warner, P. (1993) *Kids' Party Games and Activities.* Minnetonka, MN: Meadowbrook Press.

Wood, D (1988) *How Children Think and Learn.* Oxford: Basil Blackwell.

Subject Index

Note: the 'suggested games' do not cover all possibilities. Each game in this book encompasses several different foundation elements, abilities and skills.

Note: page numbers in bold refer to boxes.

Author index